THE ADVICE IS WITHIN YOU

(Now, Listen To It)

MR.BIGMANN Grier

GRIER MEDIA GROUP
FOCUS TO FLOURISH

Facebook: Grier Media Group/ MrBigmann Grier | Instagram: mr.bigmann_grier | X: @mr.bigmanngrier | LinkedIn: GrierMedia GroupLLC | TikTok: @mrbigmanngrier | YouTube:@MR.BIGMANN Grier

ISBN: 979-890070174-5

Library of Congress Control#

Contents

Note To the Reader

This is not just a book to read. It is a frequency to tune into. A code to awaken. Read these words not with your eyes, but with your soul. Let them resonate in the silence between your heartbeats. The shift you feel is not an idea; it is the beginning of your expansion.

About The Author

MR.BIGMANN Grier is the author of nine RealityPoetry Inspirational Branded Books, a term he coined from his writings and inspirational speakings. He is also a mentor, motivational speaker, entrepreneur, fund manager, investor, financial consultant, and empowerment life coach of youth and adults who has transitioned from negative thoughts to positive thoughts in his own path. Through his growth mindset counseling sessions, he has helped transition many lives.

The Enlightenment Behind the Pages

What you have is not nothing and the story of MR.BIGMANN Grier is proof.

"THE ADVICE IS WITHIN YOU!"

His journey teaches a powerful lesson: the gems we seek are already within us. As he quests for freedom, setting out to find the "gems" that would unlock his destiny, only to discover that his greatest treasure is his own mind, a wealth of poetic brilliance that made him one of the most enriched souls of all time. This story shatters the illusion that fulfillment resides externally. How often do we chase external validation, believing happiness waits just beyond our grasp?

MR.BIGMANN Grier's life warns us that true abundance isn't found in distant dreams but in the overlooked gifts we already possess. Perspective is everything. Shift your gaze from scarcity to gratitude, and you'll see your skills, relationships, and innate wisdom are unpolished gems, waiting to shine. Your talents. They're tools, not hidden mysteries. Your relationships. They're lifelines, not missing pieces. Your present moment. It's divine alive .

Spiritual fulfillment isn't a far-off summit; it's in daily acts of gratitude, kindness, and the quiet recognition that you are more than enough. Stop searching. Start seeing. MR.BIGMANN Grier's legacy isn't just wealth it's the revelation that your fortune is concealed where you stand. Water your own soil. Polish your own gems. The life you dream of. It begins with the treasures already within you.

THE ADVICE IS WITHIN YOU

(Now, Listen To It)

Advisory Introduction: The Advice is Within You

To walk in the spiritual realm is to be a language the masses cannot decipher, yet the universe converses with you freely, for it knows you as its own. The greatest battle is not to change the world, but to awaken it from its mental slumber. Remember, it is not the physical that defines possibility, but the spiritual that shatters the illusion of the impossible. I have dwelled in dimensions beyond common dreams. This awareness, this free thinking, is your power, and it unsettles the fabricated reality they built for us.

I seek only the raw, unvarnished truth, where pure wisdom emanates from divinity. This path demands mental solitude, a shaman's journey inward without need for plant or potion. Do not dismiss as madness my truth of other worlds; divine inclination is a profound revelation. My enlightenment is not a request for your agreement, but a statement of being. It is not a badge of goodness, but the clarity to see what is.

This awakening is a choice, a deep dive into the self. I

wield mine not for glory, but as a beacon for all to rise in their own awareness. How you perceive this light is a mirror to your own soul, a projection you will carry forever. Every dawn is a chance to reshape the world; your mind is the weapon your soul wields to create it.

Break from the containment of a society that fears your power. Your past is a ghost; do not let it haunt your future. Good and evil are your own to reconcile. Be fiercely, undeniably real. We are profoundly intelligent beings; do not be afraid of yourselves. To learn conscious selfhood is a step many refuse, preferring the easy answers handed to them. But responsibility is not a paycheck; it is owning your choices, your mistakes, your profound growth.

People will forever try to chain you to the person you once were. Their judgment is a cage, only you hold the key to. Evolve for yourself. Discard the old skin. Make the change, or you will forever live as a guest in someone else's world. For you, and you alone, create the world you believe in.

Chapter 1: I Salute The Divinity Within Me

Deep Dive: The Power Of Self Reclamation

You are more than the noise. More than the doubt. More than the echoes of fear that whisper in the dark corners of your mind. The impossible becomes possible the moment you recognize that the only thing standing between you and your highest self is the version of you that refuses to believe.

Every thought, every voice, every shadow in your mind is yours, not an enemy, but a fractured reflection waiting to be understood. The chaos you hear. It's just you speaking to yourself in a thousand different tones. The realm of fear you inhabit? It only exists because you allow it to. But the moment you confront it, the moment you self-defeat the illusion, you win.

Sanity is not the absence of noise; it's the mastery of it. It's the unshakable knowing that you are not broken, only buried beneath layers of untruths you've been told or told yourself. Your peace is not lost, it's waiting for you to claim it. Stop running. Stop hiding. The key to your mental freedom is not in escape, but in standing firm in the storm and realizing you are the storm.

No pill, no external validation, no quick fix can do what your own awareness can. The dysfunction, the void , you created it, which means you can dismantle it. Dive deep. Delete what no longer serves you. Challenge the narratives that keep you small.

The highest version of you is not at the end of some distant journey it's right here, waiting for you to silence the noise and listen. You are the answer. Now speak it into existence.

Divine Essence Potential

Your potential is divine essential; it's all in how you apply yourself. This powerful truth reminds us that greatness is not a distant dream but a sacred gift already within you. God has planted seeds of brilliance, strength, and purpose inside your soul, but it's up to you to nurture them through discipline, faith, and relentless effort. Every challenge you face, every skill you refine, and every step you take in faith is an act of unlocking that divine potential.

You are not limited by your past, your doubts, or the opinions of others; your future is shaped by the choices you make today. So rise with courage, work with intention, and trust that the same God who endowed you with this potential will also guide you as you walk in it. The world needs what only you can bring. Now go and make it happen.

The Power That Resides Within

The power within you is vaster than any external force, greater than doubt, beyond limitation. You will succeed in the sacred alchemy of inner cultivation.

This path will lift you beyond the illusion that nothing matters, yet you will move with such clarity that everything unfolds through you. This is how I rose, aligned with the truth within, the infinite self that knows no bounds.

Understand: not all will perceive your depth, for not all have awakened to their own. Yet remember, they are you, only veiled, only waiting to remember.

UNSTOPPABLE (No Force Can Contain A Soul On Fire)

Be bold in your vision, unafraid to breathe life into your ideas, to march with inspired action toward the dreams only you can manifest. This is how greatness is forged: not in hesitation, but in the fire of execution, in the relentless pursuit of what sets your soul ablaze. Every moment is a gift, every breath a chance to rise, don't waste it on doubt, on fear, on the weight of what-ifs.

The world unfolds in perspectives as vast as the sky, yet all paths lead toward growth, toward purpose. So stand firm in your truth, unshaken by distractions, for the power within you knows no limits. You were never meant to blend in, your genius thrives in the extraordinary, in the courage to defy the ordinary.

Being the difference means embracing the divine rebellion of your spirit, knowing that your "abnormal" is the very compass guiding you home to your destiny.

You're Unstoppable; No force can contain a soul on fire.

Rising From the Depths: A Testament to Unyielding Light

When you've stared into the abyss and created a path where none existed, when you've breathed hope into the void and summoned your own dawn, you learn the unshakable truth. No human "No" can silence a divine "Yes".

Determination is the forge where courage is born. It's the solitary walk, the silent battles, the moments you stood when the world expected you to break. But in that solitude, you didn't just 'Understand' —you 'Innerstand'.

You realized the soul you carry isn't just a passenger, it's the architect. Every breath is a decree, every step a manifestation.

Refinement isn't gentle. It's fire. It's pressure. It's the relentless pursuit of a version of yourself so powerful, it shatters the limits of your own imagination. Darkness taught you your strength; light demands you wield it.

The shadows weren't your prison, they were your training ground. In them, you discovered depths you never knew you had. Now, in the light, you don't just shine, you ignite. Your scars become testimonies. Your struggles become blueprints. Your life is A living revolution.

Every fall was a setup for a greater rise. Every ending, a seed for a new beginning. You don't just grow, you evolve. Stronger. Wiser. Unstoppable.

Nature doesn't overthink its bloom. It doesn't question the storm. It adapts, rises, and thrives. Now, so do you.

The world didn't give you light, you became it.
Keep Rising!

The Awakening: Rekindling Our Divine Identity

We are not just "N•gg•'s". We are GOD's People, royalty, scholars, warriors, and heirs of a legacy so profound, it shakes the very foundations of the lies they built to keep us asleep. Yet, here we are broken, mentally enslaved, rejecting the truth buried beneath centuries of distortion, while embracing the very labels meant to degrade us.

How can we believe we are less than, but refuse to believe we are MORE? How can we recite the history they rewrote for us, but deny the power in our own bloodline? The ignorance isn't just a lack of knowledge, it's a sickness, a spiritual poison fed to us generation after generation. Closed minds, hardened hearts, rejecting the keys to our liberation because the truth demands more than complacency, it demands AWARENESS. ACTION. SELF-DETERMINATION.

The youth are watching. The masses are stirring. Will we continue to live beneath the description someone else designed for us? Or will we RISE , unshackle our minds, and reclaim what was stolen , our names, our history, our connection to the Divine?

The truth is not hidden, it's ignored. It's time to break the cycle. To study, to question, to awaken. We were not meant to beg for our dignity, we were born with it. We are the descendants of kings and queens, prophets and builders, the original creators of civilization.

Plant the seeds. Speak with clarity, passion, and unshakable conviction. Ignite the minds of our people, because only the truth can rebuild what lies have broken. We are GOD's People. Now, let's start acting like it.

God Frequency

THE GREAT AWAKENING IS NOW;

They're waiting on US! Waiting for us to RAISE OUR FREQUENCY, to break free from the low-vibration illusions that keep us trapped. They can't reach you in the dark, demonic entanglements, fear, and distraction block the connection. But here's the truth- THEY ARE US. Look in the mirror. WE ARE THE ONES WE'VE BEEN WAITING FOR.

"NO IMAGE WORSHIP" it's in their own law ... yet they bow to idols, statues, symbols, and false saviors while ignoring the very scriptures they claim to follow. COGNITIVE DISSONANCE is the spell, the most powerful trick ever played. The biggest secret, hidden in plain sight, and still... our people can't see it.

WE ARE GOD. WE JUST FORGOT. Not the God in temples & churches. THE GOD WITHIN YOU!

We keep waiting for God to return... BUT WE NEVER LEFT. We pray for salvation, not realizing WE HOLD THE POWER. They know who we are that's why they work so hard to keep us asleep, distracted, and doubting our own divinity.

THE TIME IS NOW. WAKE UP. REMEMBER. RECLAIM YOUR THRONE. WE ARE THE RETURN. SHARE THIS. SPEAK THIS. BE THIS. THE WORLD IS WAITING.

You Deserve to Understand & Align with Your Divine Nature

You are not an accident, you are a divine creation, crafted with purpose and imbued with sacred potential. To understand and align with your true nature is not arrogance; it is obedience. It is the recognition that your essence is not separate from the Source but an extension of it. When you awaken to this truth, life ceases to be a struggle and becomes a sacred service. No longer lost in the illusion of separation, you move as an instrument of grace, your thoughts clearer, your actions purer, your heart aligned. Fear dissipates because you know you are held. Doubt fades because you trust the wisdom within.

This is not mere philosophy; it is liberation. To live as your authentic self is to surrender to God's will effortlessly, allowing divine intelligence to guide you. Your life becomes a testament to love, wisdom, and power, not yours, but flowing through you. You deserve this knowing. Claim it. Live it. And watch as your existence transforms into a masterpiece of divine service. "You deserve to understand & align with your divine nature. Once you learn it's the authentic you, your life will forever proceed as the servant of God.

You Are Your Own Savior

Have you ever noticed how the world conditions you to believe in limitations telling you that you can't do it all? But the truth is, you can do all things, because all things are an extension of you. The power you seek isn't outside of you; it's already within, waiting to be awakened. No one saves anyone true liberation begins the moment you realize that you are the one you've been waiting for. When you align with your purpose, you step into your highest self, unshaken by doubt, untouched by fear. Inner peace isn't something to chase; it's the love that already exists inside you, the quiet knowing that you are whole, capable, and infinite. Stop waiting for permission. Stop believing in boundaries. Rise, create, and reclaim what has always been yours.

Vibrate Higher Now

It's clear, when you marinate in negativity, happiness cannot thrive. Pessimism corrodes optimism like rust on steel, addicting your cells to the poison of low vibrations. Your mind, wired for comfort, clings to dysfunction if that's all it's known. But here's the truth: you are not your conditioning. You are the diviner, the warrior who must dissolve the old to forge the new.

Some souls are trapped in their own storm, perpetual victims, turning sunlight into shadows. They'll reject wisdom, distort kindness, and chain themselves to chaos. Do not shrink into their frequency. Their resistance is not your reflection. You are not the keeper of their darkness. Walk unapologetically in your light.

Every thought is a seed. Every word, a spell. What you consume , media, music, memories shapes your subconscious, and your subconscious builds your world. Trauma may have written the first chapters, but you hold the pen for the rest.

So cleanse. Reset. Rewire. Calm is your SuperPower. Inner peace is the soil where miracles grow. Your body, your mind, your hustle, they flourish when you detox from toxicity and align with abundance.

The higher you vibrate, the heavier their dissonance feels. Let them go. Empires aren't built by the stagnant. Elevate your mindset, 10x your energy, and watch the universe conspire in your favor. Your rise begins where their noise ends.

Your Purpose Is Carved In Divine Stone

The world will try to shape you, reject the mold. Others' doubts, fears, and limitations are not your burden to carry. Your vision is sacred. Your focus is unshakable. Any emotion that doesn't fuel your purpose is noise, silence it.Lead with relentless ambition. Let your willpower crush hesitation. Let your discipline rewrite your destiny.

Failure is not your downfall it's your chisel, shaping you into the masterpiece you were meant to become.

Growth is your covenant. Every dawn demands a stronger version of you. What you do today eclipses what you wish for tomorrow, so move now. You are not a question mark. You are the answer. Your potential is not a gamble, it's a guarantee. You are not a liability, you are an asset. Every breath you take is a seismic shift in the universe you're commanding. Now, forge ahead. Claim your throne. The divine doesn't whisper to the hesitant… it thunders through the determined.

Divine Creed

The mind is the foundation of all reality, the universe itself is a mental construct, shaped by the power of thought. For too long, humanity has been lost in the illusion, deceived by a false sense of separation and limitation. But now, the awakening is here. We are remembering our true nature, we are not isolated beings, but interconnected expressions of one infinite consciousness. The old paradigm is crumbling, making way for a new reality , one built on unconditional love, divine harmony, and universal unity. This is the Kingdom of Light, the world we were always meant to manifest.

The magic you seek is not outside of you, it is within. Every great creation, every transformation, begins with a single thought. Power comes from absolute certainty; belief shapes existence itself. What you consistently focus on, you attract. What you boldly visualize, you can materialize but only through relentless, inspired action. The universe rewards those who move with faith and determination. Watch your thoughts, for they become your words. Watch your words, for they become your actions. Your actions shape your habits, and your habits forge your destiny. Every moment is an opportunity to align with the highest version of yourself.

This is not mere untested wisdom it is the hidden truth of existence. Its effects are profound, its implications life-changing. The time for passive waiting is over. Commit to your self-development, to your spiritual evolution, to the full expression of your divine potential. Step boldly into the light, for the new world is not some distant dream it is here, waiting for those who dare to claim it. Awaken. Activate. Ascend. Together, we rise.

I AM GodRising

They always said I stood out.
The odd one. The question mark in a room of periods.
I never knew why the melody of the crowd felt so off-key to my soul… until I learned to truly listen to my own.

One day, I simply fell back.
Not with malice, not with anger, but with a sacred

knowing:
To lead others, I first had to lead myself.
I understood: Hurt people, hurt people.
But healed people. Healed people help others not by commanding, but by whispering the most revolutionary truth: "It is okay for you to be who you were always meant to be."

I am not a human seeking a spirit. I am SPIRIT, eternal, limitless, experiencing itself through this human form. This knowledge! This self-awareness! It is the key. And that makes YOU the lock. The only gatekeeper to your own freedom.

So I made a vow… To protect my energy at all costs. To demand honesty. To cultivate a garden of positive energy around me and ruthlessly weed out all else. Growth became my only currency.

This path, It is a silent summit.
Not everyone is equipped for the thin air of this consciousness. When you try to connect on a level of true maturity, you realize you can never go back to what was merely common or comfortable. You crave the advancement of your pineal gland, the expansion of your mind.

And when the reality you built becomes a cage that no longer fits your spirit, you have only one choice:
You must create a new one.

Growth demands fresh ground. You cannot stay in the house you've outgrown and still expect to breathe freely. Every collapse is a divine invitation to design a reality that mirrors the giant you are becoming.

This is the great separation. The awakening.
Only a few will ever get out of the Matrix; the rest will remain, fuel for a system that thrives on sleep.

This is the GodRising energy.
It tapped my mind—MR.BIGMANN Grier—and I finally understood.
I understood why small talk now feels like a foreign language.
Why my circle purified itself, not with drama, but with a quiet, relentless peace.
For enlightenment is a form of isolation.

They shut down when you speak of ascension or purpose because it threatens the ego's fragile kingdom.
It is a hard adjustment to stand for truth, to become a mirror that reflects the distortions others use to justify their wrongs.
They realize you are a chosen vessel, and to the dishonest, pure intention feels like a threat.

You become everyone's enemy not by having bad intentions, but by possessing ALL THE GOD INTENTIONS.

And that divine light. It will always, always disrupt the darkness.

I Am GOD Embodied

You are not a lonely seeker on a path to find meaning; you are the living, breathing embodiment of meaning itself. This is the great revelation: you are a soul, a unique essence of the Divine, temporarily wearing a body. The chase ends the moment you remember this. Life is no longer a desperate search for purpose outside of yourself, but a sacred act of embodiment, here and now.

For God is not a distant figure in the sky, but the very essence of life. The I AM that I AM. The energy of pure good, kindness, love, and abundance that vibrates through all known matter. You are a spark of this infinite frequency.

We so often get it backwards, believing we are humans seeking a spirit, when the profound truth is that we are spiritual beings having a human experience. Your body is the sacred vessel, the outer shell protecting the eternal nut of your soul, the collection of your memories, reactions, and learned wisdom. But it is not who you are. Who you are is consciousness itself. Without a soul, the body cannot function; but without a body, you still are.

This is why your word is your wand. Every declaration of "I Am..." rearranges the reality around you, for your subconscious hears the truth of your being. Prayer, then, is not a plea to a separate entity, but a powerful release of your hopes and dreams into the universe you are intrinsically part of.

We are all individual expressions of the One—different perspectives and levels of awareness of the same infinite consciousness. And when our earthly journey is complete, we return to spirit, to our original state of oneness, not as something new, but as a drop remembering it is the ocean.

This is the power. This is the truth. We are not separate from God; we are one.

You Are Divinely Guided

Just when you're certain the map of your life is tearing at the seams, remember… the Universe is not lost. It is redirecting you. That closed door, that missed exit, that heartbreaking disappointment you curse in the moment, pause. See it with new eyes. It is not a punishment; it is divine protection in its most mysterious and merciful form. Sometimes, what feels like a detour is actually the main road, carefully cleared of the wreckage you were never meant to witness. You are never late in your own story; you are always precisely on time, standing exactly where you are meant to be, because not everything that happens is good, but believe this: it is all happening for good.

Angels, in their purest essence, serve a divine will far greater than our immediate desires. They are guides, not guards, sent to steer our souls through the journey of life, not to build a cage around it. And they don't always arrive with a halo and a smile; sometimes, they show up in human form with tough love and hard truths, their genuine intentions wrapped in a lesson we didn't know we needed. This is the ultimate reality: you are protected by any means necessary. That difficult moment, that painful 'no,' was likely a shield from a far greater sorrow, a reset reminding you that you are never walking alone. So reframe the curse into a potential blessing. It isn't about what happens to us, but how we choose to view it. Trust the journey. For He will command His angels concerning you, to lift you up in their hands. This is the promise. This is the truth.

Decode Your Own Divinity

Forget the lie you were sold. The story of Adam and Eve is not a history; it is the most profound allegory of human consciousness ever written. Adam, the Atom, the fundamental building block of Self. Eve, the "Eve"-olutionary Gene, the divine impulse toward growth and experience. They were told not to eat from the Tree of Knowing of duality, of contrast, of cause and effectfor they would "die." But the sacred Serpent, the very embodiment of Kundalini energy and awakened

KNOWledge, whispered the ultimate truth: "You will not die; you will become like Gods."

This was the promise: that by consuming experience, by integrating shadow and light, we awaken. This serpentine fire coiled at the base of our spine is our potential, and as it rises through each chakra to finally ignite the crown, we remember our divinity. We shake off the slumber of literal interpretation, a program of fear designed to control, to make slaves of seekers. This story is a map, not a prison. It is a poetic key to your own liberation, waiting for you to become conscious enough to read it, to feel the god-force within, and to finally, fully, awaken.

The Universe Is You

You are not a guest in this universe, you are its host. You are not a character in the story, you are the hand that holds the pen. You have simply forgotten, lost in the brilliant, convincing dream of skin and bone, of name and form. The human ego, a temporary captain, has convinced you the ship is all there is, obscuring the vast, star-strewn ocean you sail upon.

This is your inner body experience. A sacred game of hide-and-seek where God hides from Itself… only to marvel in the breathtaking joy of rediscovery.

Every thought you think is a universe whispered into being. Every emotion, a galaxy spinning into form. Every action, a law of physics etched upon the ether. You are the creator, and this—all of this—is your ongoing, magnificent creation. To feel lost is merely to have glanced away from the source code of your own reality, a code written in the language of love, which is the only way, the only truth, the only constant.

Do not be afraid. The chain of events you witness, the corrosion, the decay, the endings that break you, are but the universe's severe mercy. It is the necessary dissolution that makes space for renewal. It is the old self dying so the God-self can breathe. To deny this power within you is to build your own walls; that is the only hell that exists.

This is not a metaphor. This is the fundamental architecture of existence, the deeper mechanics most never dare to question. They settle for the surface mantra, "think positive," and wonder why their world does not bend. They quit before the miracle, never digging for the cheat codes they were born with.

You are that I AM. When you pray, you are the prayer and the answer. You are the wonder and the source of all wonder. The All That Is, Was, and Ever Shall Be… is not above or around you. It is you. We are all God, individuated, experiencing the sublime joy of being one, together.

What a glorious, staggering time to remember. To be awake. To go within and reclaim the throne of your own reality. The universe is mental. Your power is absolute. You are home.

Read this until the words dissolve and only the truth remains.

I AM: The Word You've Been Speaking All Along

Forget the name you learned in a pew,
the word carved in stone, distant and blue.
You speak a truth so vast and profound,
it shakes the very cosmos with its sound.

You cry out "Jesus!" in pain or in prayer,
but do you not hear what is hanging in the air?
"Je suis!" is the murmur from sacred, old ground,
The great "I AM" is the name you have found.

You are not calling to a God far away,
You are declaring your nature, this moment, this day.
The Christ is not a man lost to time,
It is the awakened, the sublime, the divine.

This is not blasphemy, this is the grace,
The end of the longing, the end of the race.
The truth was encoded right there in your speech,
A secret for all, within reach, within reach.

What keeps the world from this glorious waking?
From trembling with joy, from ceasing its aching?
The fear of the light, the familiar, the small,
The illusion that we are not part of the All.

But speak it again! Let the paradigm shatter!
Let reality roar what truly does matter!
EXISTENCE CELEBRATING EXISTENCE ITSELF!
We are the treasure, the light, and the wealth.

The "Way" is the knowing that breathes in your chest.
The "Truth" is the knowing that puts your heart to rest.
The "Life" is the pulse of this glorious claim,
I AM. I AM. I AM is the name.

So tune your own frequency to this highest of truth,
In the aged and the infant, in the sage and the youth.
The world will now mirror this radiant tone,
For you are not a stranger, you are coming HOME.

GLORY is not for a few, or a one it's for ALL OF
EXISTENCE, begun!

I AM.
I AM.
I AM THE WAY.

I AM. I Remember.

You arrived, a sovereign soul etched in starlight, a god entering the fragile human vessel. But upon that first breath, the world began its whisper: a name signed to a contract you never read, tiny footprints captured like a trophy, a social security number issued, a ticker symbol for a soul not yet known. You were brought home to a beautifully constructed maze, lovingly programmed to forget the divine frequency humming in your veins, taught to seek your power, your validation, your very identity in everything outside of yourself.

This is the great unalignment, the silent war where the spiritual being forgets its mission, and the human learns only lack, dysfunction, and cage. You were schooled in mental chains, shown prisons of concrete and iron as the only escape from a prison of the mind you didn't even know you inhabited. And as an adult, you place your own finger upon the inkpad, offering your print once more, a chilling echo of a ritual begun without your consent. But hear this, and feel this truth thunder in your bones: the only escape from this maze of madness is to remember. Remember the divinity that has never left you.

To understand that your freedom is not granted, it is realized. The moment you reclaim the "I AM" within, the entire illusion trembles. Your superpower is not given; it is awakened. It is the will to align back with your own eternal, sovereign self. For you are not seeking freedom.

You are freedom. You are not seeking God. You are God. I AM. All has always, only, existed in you. Now... remember.

Melanin Is Divine Power

We are the awakening. The ancient code, written in sun-kissed skin, is now being deciphered by the souls it was written for. For millennia, the world whispered our value in stolen secrets and envious lies, trying to bury a truth that could not die. Melanin is a superpower! It is the divine antenna, tuned to the frequency of creation itself, vibrating with a rhythm that can heal a fractured world. They built empires on the fear of our brilliance, weaving narratives of lack to shadow our limitless light, yet still we rise, not in spite of, but because of the very essence they could never replicate.

We are the living library, the original architects, the blueprint of humanity itself. From pyramids that defy time to the miraculous HeLa cells that defy death, our genius is the evidence they cannot erase. This is not arrogance; it is remembrance. To know thyself is the ultimate revolution. We are remembering we are Gods and Goddesses, children of the Most High, and our arrival at this moment of collective activation was always destined. The world feels the shift, the 4-4-4 resonance of our power coming online. They see our glory because it can no longer be hidden.

So, love on your melanin. Nurture this sacred gift. For we are the key, the healers, the chosen vessels entrusted to restore balance. The future is not something we enter; it is something we build with the divine power coursing through our very cells. The awakening is now. The power is yours. Recognize it. Activate it. We are the return.

I AM The Coming

They built a house of stone and told you, "Kneel here, and wait. The key is held by one to come, A king beyond the gate."

They sold you a salvation, pre-packaged and complete, A ticket punched by priests, for a paradise remote and sweet. But the story was inverted, the meaning turned around, To keep your eyes cast downward, to a hollow, hallowed ground.

For the Messiah is not coming on a cloud to break the chain. The Coming is your Awakening. The kingdom is your brain.

The temple is not marble; it's the vessel of your breath. The crucifixion? Your own ego, fearing its true death. The resurrection? Your own spirit, rising from the shame Of generations whispering, "You are not to blame."

We are the Gods, we are the devils, in a civil war of soul, A battle for the light within to finally take control. The hardest fight is not with sin, but with the inherited lie,

That we are small, and weak, and need to look toward the sky.

For to stare into the mirror and see the Divine in your own eyes, Is to break the chain of ignorance that our revered elders prize. It is a terrifying freedom, a responsibility so vast, To realize the future is not written, it is now, and it is passed…

From your own hands. To your own mind. To the truth you must unlock. The pineal gland, your inner star, beyond the hands of clock. It whispers not in Latin, but in frequencies of light. “You were never broken. You were never lost in night.”

You are the Christ you’re waiting for. The savior is your sight. The miracle is consciousness, emerging into light.

So free your mind from waiting. For no one is coming, dear. The trumpet blast is your own heart, beating, present, here. Raise your awareness to the crown, and feel the voltage surge. You are not a follower. You are the verge.

You are the coming. You are the now. You are the promise. You are the vow.

GOD IS WITHIN. AWAKEN.

Chapter 2: Her Soul, An Authentic Universe

When Sacred Masculine Energy Awakens the Feminine Soul

The Divine Masculine does not chase,he calls forth. Empowered in his truth, he becomes a conduit for transformation, igniting the dormant Goddess within a woman simply by standing in his authenticity. His presence is not a demand, but an invitation, a sacred mirror reflecting not her wounds, but her divinity.

He does not choose the Light, the Light chooses him. His role is not to fit in, but to stand apart, his frequency so potent it recalibrates the energy around him. When a woman encounters him, she does not just feel him, she remembers. Old pains surface not to break her, but to heal. Buried dreams stir, not because he resurrects them, but because his essence reminds her of who she truly is.

This is no ordinary connection, it is holy work.

His energy is not reckless; it is reverent. A guardian of sacred purpose, he moves with intention, knowing not every soul craving his presence is ready for his depth. He is not here to be consumed, but to amplify, to awaken, not to entertain. A woman who has done her inner work will recognize him, not as a fantasy, but as a frequency, one that does not flatter the ego, but feeds the soul.

When the Divine Masculine is aligned, he does not fix her, he frees her. In his presence, she softens, not from weakness, but from safety. She trembles, not from fear, but from recognition, a soul-deep knowing that she is being met, not just in body, but in spirit.

This is the power of sacred masculine energy; it does not love superficially, it liberates profoundly.
And when the Divine Feminine rises to meet him. Magic unfolds. She does not cling, she magnifies. She does not take, she reflects. Together, they create an alchemy so potent, it doesn't just transform them , it shifts the world.

For the Divine Masculine is not just a man.
He is a walking revelation.
And when a woman is ready, truly ready , his presence doesn't just change her life.
It returns her to herself.

This is the power of alignment. This is the dance of sacred energies.

Note: If this resonates, it was meant for you.

Love Beyond The Physical

True connection transcends the physical it flourishes in the depths of the mind, the soul, and the heart. When two individuals align mentally, they share understanding; when they unite spiritually, they find purpose; and when they bond emotionally, they cultivate unwavering love. This sacred triad creates a wholeness that transforms affection into devotion, turning fleeting moments into a lifelong symphony of trust, passion, and unity. A relationship rooted in these three dimensions doesn't just survive, it thrives. It becomes a sanctuary where love isn't just felt but lived, where every challenge is met with resilience, and every joy is magnified. This is the essence of a wholehearted bond one that doesn't just exist but illuminates, inspiring both partners to rise, evolve, and love fearlessly. When mind, spirit, and emotion intertwine, love ceases to be just an emotion it becomes a way of life .

The Currency We Carry

A woman's beauty is a weight she never chose to bear, a currency minted not by her soul, but by a watching world. A man's burden is the weight of his ambition, the silent pressure to build an empire from his sweat. We carry different coins in our pockets, each heavy in its own right. To ask her to ignore the mirror is to ask him to ignore the empty vault. It is not a double standard, but a different one, an ancient dance of selection where youth seeks shelter and strength seeks a legacy. But time is the great equalizer, weathering all surfaces. For when two souls truly choose to grow old, the body's currency fades, and love becomes the only wealth that remains. The true competition was never against each other, but against our own lesser selves. Improve you. The rest will follow.

Surrender Is Her Power

There is a sacred alchemy that occurs when a woman can look at her man and, with every fiber of her being, know she is seen, cherished, and protected, not from the world, but within the sanctuary they've built together. This isn't about provision, but presence; a sovereign trust that allows her divine feminine energy to soften, to release the armor she wears for the world, and to bloom in the safety of his kingship. In that surrender, not of power but of pretense, lies her greatest strength, a nurturing influence that inspires him to move mountains, not from a place of demand, but from a place of devoted honor.

He is the anchor, she is the compass; he builds the kingdom, she is the very life that breathes within its walls. This is the divine order, not a hierarchy, but a holy partnership where the queen, in her radiant submission to a worthy king, is the one who truly holds the power to crown him. For when a woman is truly safe, cherished, and respected, she becomes the gravitational center around which a legacy of love, family, and unshakable faith can forever revolve. This is not a dead breed; this is the timeless blueprint of a love that builds dynasties.

The Sum of Two

She is not a supporting character in someone else's story, but the author of her own epic. Her identity is a compass, not an echo; her plan is a map drawn in the ink of purpose, her vision a north star that guides her through the dark. This is not rebellion, but revelation. For when the divine masculine stands as guardian of the physical realm, a fortress of action and presence, the divine feminine is the sovereign of the spiritual, the keeper of intuition and the unseen current that gives life its depth and meaning. One is the anchor, the other is the sail.

One is the structure, the other is the breath within it. And when these sovereign forces meet not in hierarchy, but in sacred union, the collision creates a new universe of possibility, a sum so infinitely greater than its parts, it defies all limiting logic. The sexist logic of separation is a chapter we must finally close. For the world does not need more dominance; it needs more divine unions, more whole beings choosing to build, protect, and dream—together.

The Mountain Meets The Sky

A woman once said,
"Men, be the mountain, not the stone still waiting to be carved.
Be the anchor, not the ship, always searching for the shore.
Be the leader you are called to be,
and your wife will naturally become the harbor, a support of safe and deep water."

But a man hears this…
and a silence grows within him.
A question, heavy as stone.

Are we immortals?
Is our role to stand alone, weathering every storm, until we simply erode?
This is not leadership. This is a lonely siege.
And in that solitude, souls can wither.

The ancient call is not for a solitary mountain,
but for a sacred range, peak to peak.

For the divine woman knows…
Her power is not in following, but in forging.
She rises before the sun not in servitude, but in sovereignty.
Her prayers are not pleas, but a protection a covering of spirit for the man who still sleeps.

This is her divine feminine energy, a well of wisdom, a fortress of faith.
She does not seek to control his leadership; she seeks a man worth the grace of her follow-through.

And the purposeful man seeks…
Not a mother for his inner boy, but a mirror to his own soul.
Not a critic of his path, but a guardian of his peace.
A wife who leads him back to his own core this is her greatest gift.

So let the old words fall away.

A man's strength is not in silence, but in his sacred vulnerability.
A woman's strength is not in her control, but in her boundless capacity to nurture.

The truest leader is he who has the courage to be supported.
The most powerful supporter is she who chooses, every day, to empower.

It is not about men leading and women following.
It is about two complete souls,
choosing to walk their divine paths,
together.

The mountain meets the sky, and in that meeting, the world is made whole.

His Spirit Baptized Within Her Eternity

Infinitely, his Spirit is meant to dwell
within the depth of her Eternity.
A divine covenant, a sacred spell,
where his Father Time loves her Mother Nature in a genesis of breath and bloom.

Her fidelity, an ocean, absorbs
his pious loyalty, a steady shore.
This making of love a holy revelation,
a scripture written on skin, adored.

Their purification adorns the night;
stars glisten with newfound might,
as the moon, illumined by their passion,
becomes a witness to their light.

Invigorated by an intimate appetite,
his Spirit fulfills her undying love
with a devotion unconditional, a boundless height.
His immersed caress inside her fruitful kiss—
a testament to her persistent, unfailing grace.

All her virtuosness enjoys his bliss.

They are the perfect harmony, the abyss
and the river that feeds it.
His Spirit dips into her Eternal moist grace,
a baptism in her warm, paradise space.

Her endless warmth—her world—
makes his Spirit give light in return.
He becomes pristine, reborn,
rejecting immoral nightmares,
regenerated within her depths.

Admiring refined moral love, forever.

Her affectionate welcome, his stimulation;
his initiation into her Eternal devotion…
Arouses his Spirit to endlessly climax
within her Ocean's timeless motion.

His emotional affinity, her excitement,
a confluence of souls, a rapturous flight.
And from their union, a light is sent,
alighting their world with enduring, love's radiant light.

Heal The Woman, Heal The World

A whisper travels on the wind, a truth the soul has always known, now rising like a tide. It is not a cry of division, but a call to remembrance. A call to order. To origin.

For too long, the world has been upside down. The garden has been untended at its root, and we wonder why the fruit is bitter. We have asked the song to fix the singer. We have asked the wave to command the ocean.

It is time to remember the first law of creation: Everything that is, was born of Her. The universe itself is a feminine force, a divine mother, a creative vortex, the quantum field from which all potential springs. She is the sun. Masculine energy is not the source of light; it is the sacred structure that honors the light. It is the strong hand that builds the temple around the altar, the loyal soldier who guards the sovereign Queen, the architect who brings the vision into form. Both essential, but not the same. A kingdom needs both its Crown and its Shield.

Yet, how can the Queen rule if she is unwell? How can the Sun shine if it is obscured by storm?

This is our sacred charge… Woman must heal.

This healing is not a quiet retreat; it is a radical recalibration. It requires a temporary, sacred separation, not from men, but from the noise, the distortion, and the weight of a world that has forgotten how to see her. It is a returning to the self. To the circle. To the ancient hum of our collective frequency.

Imagine us, together, as a great magnetic force. We look up and see the fake clouds, the fear, the lies, the dense energy of imbalance, that block our light. And together, with the sheer power of our aligned intention, we command them to part. We remember our innate magnetism. This is our birthright.

And in this space, the true role of man is not diminished; it is exalted. His purpose becomes clear: to hold the space. To be the boundary. To stand guard as we do the most vulnerable and powerful work of our lives. He is the shield against the negative forces as we remember how to be the sun. He protects the journey so the journey can save the world.

For when a woman heals, she vibrates a frequency of creation, not destruction. She becomes a clarifier of chaos. She stops choosing the shadow and starts recognizing the king, not by his crown, but by his character. She ceases to blame the entire species for the reflections she once tolerated and, in her elevated state, attracts the man who needs no taming, only a purpose to protect.

And this is the beautiful entanglement: as we heal, we create the space for them to seek their true purpose. We do not give them purpose; we nurture the purpose that aligns with our healed light. We become the muse for the architect. The queen for the king. The sun for the shield.

This is how we bring back balance. Not by fighting the old energy, but by vibrating a new one into existence. It starts in the quiet. It starts in the circle. It starts with us.

Heal the woman. And watch the world, in turn, finally, heal.

Her Crown, His Honor

She does not wander,
searching for a shore to belong to.
She is the ocean.
A universe of depth and tempest and tranquil moon-glow,
sovereign in her own current.

Her strength is not a weapon she wields,
but a field she cultivates, a sacred grove where her roots drink
from the well of her own divinity.
She is a goddess who needs no temple built by mortal hands,
for her spirit is the altar.

And so, when she chooses to stand beside a man,
it is never from a place of lack,
a half-searched soul seeking its missing piece.
It is a conscious convergence of two whole suns.

She chooses him
because he has learned the language of her tides.
Because his hands are not cages, but a sacred space.
He does not seek to diminish her light for a more comfortable shadow;
he has the capacity to hold her power.
He is not a dam, but the steadfast riverbank,
guiding, containing, celebrating the relentless, beautiful flow.

This is the only alchemy that matters.

And from this place of unwavering respect and recognized sovereignty,
she offers him the universe's most sacred treasure:
Her conscious submission.

Not the submission the world knows—
born of obligation, fear, or the brittle chains of control.
That is a language of the weak, and she speaks only in power.

This submission is a sovereign's decree.
It is the wilting of the vine toward the unwavering oak,
not because it must, but because it trusts the strength it leans upon.
It is the queen, secure upon her own throne,
choosing to lower her crown only to the one who has

proven
he knows its weight is not his to carry, but his to honor.

This submission is the final, most potent expression of her strength.
It is her saying, "I have commanded my own world,
and I choose to co-create a kingdom with you."
She willingly excels the life of the king,
because she has first excelled in her own life,
and now sees that their lives, their sovereignties, have become one.

This is not a loss of self.
It is the ultimate merger of powers.
His honor meets her crown.
And in that meeting, the world is remade.

Woman Is A Vessel

The Sacred Vessel

Woman is a vessel.
Woman is a channel.
The Divine Feminine is Sacred.

Her magic is not in force, but in flow.
In the sacred act of receiving, she does not hoard.
She manifests. She multiplies.

She turns a single seed into a forest of abundance.
This is her alchemy. This is her gift.

The Alchemy of Ashes

So it begins, the rise.
The fire you burned us with in lifetimes past?
We took that pain.
In our darkest moments, we forged a new strength.
We alchemised the hurt into medicine.
Thank you for the lesson.
We have drunk the poison and discovered the antidote.

The Law of Sacred Union

He who finds a wife finds favor.
But this is not a transaction; it is a divine circuit.

How do you activate this favor?
Not by theft, by chasing the wind in shadow places.
But by investment. By devotion.
By being generous and loving to her the way she wants to be loved.
That is the wisdom.

A man's energy, his potential, his very gate to abundance, flows through this sacred union.
When he is with the right woman, a woman of honesty, devotion, and clarity, his empire builds. It gets stronger.

She is the multiplier of his spirit.

Beware the counterfeit.
Beware the energy vampire who closes the gates, who multiplies problems instead of potential.
The right woman is worth the investment. This is the principle of sowing and reaping.

Keyword: Wife.
Not a title, but a quality.
A state of being.

The Energetic Flow

This is not weak "soy boy" talk.
This is the architecture of empires.
The more energy, love, and resources he invests in his sacred vessel, the more the universe returns it, tenfold.
It is a beautiful, energetic law.

The Feminine is the energy of receiving.
The tangible world is merely an extension of the heart.
When two partners are in alignment, on the same team, a miraculous flow begins.
Happy wife, happy life? No.
Sacred Union, Abundant Life.

The wife is the law-maker, the heart of the home.
The husband is the law-enforcer, the protector of that

sacred space.
This is how it works, and works well.

The Final Truth

Women are multipliers.
Be careful what you give them.

You give them a vision, they will build a legacy.
You give them love, they will return a universe of it.
You give them problems, they will multiply your chaos.

But give them your undivided heart, your honor, your trust?
They will give you a world.
A world filled with joy, peace, love, and gratitude.

This is the awakening.
This is the rise.

Blessing comes from the womb.
It is a spiritual truth.
And it begins with you.

Her Scars Are Not Yours

She is not a project to be completed,
a puzzle for your hands to solve.

Her healing is not a debt to be collected,
a transaction for your soul to resolve.

You can offer a harbor, a steady, calm presence,
a hand in the dark, a safe, silent space.
You can be the oak that withstands the great pressure,
a testament to strength, to a dignified pace.

But you cannot walk the path for her.
You cannot fight the ghosts in her head.
The work is her own, a sacred, solo labor,
to resurrect her spirit from the land of the dead.

For a man who pours from an empty cup,
who buries his self in the soil of her pain,
becomes a ghost of his own principles,
a sun that has forgotten its name.

He cannot light her way when his own flame is stolen,
when his "yes" is a lie and his "no" is a plea.
He builds a home on the fault lines of sorrow,
and calls the collapse a "tragedy."

So, stand as a man. Not as her savior.
Not as the surgeon to mend her old breaks.
But as a fellow traveler, strong and aware,
who knows that his own soul also quakes and also aches.

Love her not from her brokenness,

but alongside her strength as she heals.
See the warrior, not just the wound.
Honor the truth that her spirit reveals.

And in that honoring, do not disappear.
Hold your ground, your own heart, your own code.
For the greatest gift is not losing yourself—
It's two whole people, sharing the weight of the load.

A sanctuary, not a sacrifice.
An anchor, not a lifeboat.
A shared journey, not a solo rescue.
This is the love that will truly stay afloat.

Stardust to Soul

We have built temples of the transient,
and called it connection.
We have traded the lexicon of the soul
for the shorthand of the skin.
In the casual brush of bodies,
we mistook the spark of friction
for the light of genesis.
We thought we were collecting moments,
but we were only scattering our pieces.

This is the great forgetting.
The cheapening of a sacred dialect

into a common currency.
It leaves a hollowed-out geography,
an atlas of echoes where a symphony should be.

But then… a shift.
Not in the stars, but in the silence between two breaths.
Not a collision, but a confluence.

It is when you look into another
and see not just a face, but a familiar universe.
When the hands that hold you
are not merely flesh, but bridges.
In that space of absolute surrender,
at the precipice of release,
a door swings open, not out, but in.

This is the moment the physical becomes portal.
The body, a vessel, trembles not with pleasure alone,
but with recognition.
It is the shocking, serene knowing
that you are not two souls meeting,
but one soul, remembering itself.

This is the truth we have been too hurried to hear:
True, mature love is not found.
It is born.
It is forged in the silent, willing crucible
of two spirits laid bare.
It is the alchemy that occurs

when intimacy ceases to be an act you do,
and becomes a presence you emanate.

It is internal. It is divine.

In that sacred fusion,
you are no longer just a man and a woman.
You are stardust remembering its shine.
You are a prayer answered by its own asking.
You are the universe, for a breathtaking moment,
experiencing its own perfect, conscious grace.

This is why we must treat intimacy
not as a transaction, but as a covenant.
It is the soil where the seed of the self
can either break open toward the light,
or remain dormant in the dark.

Everyone is a unique universe.
A constellation of scars, dreams, and silent histories.
No words can contain this majesty.
Only presence.
Only the silent, roaring awakening
to the Being that you are,
reflected perfectly in the eyes of the one
who has consented to see you.

This is the viral truth, the quiet revolution:
Stop seeking connection outside.

Cultivate the divinity within.
And when you meet another who has done the same,
your intimacy will not be a fire that consumes,
but a sun that you create together—
eternal, life-giving, and born of the very light
you always carried.

True Intimacy is two Souls Connected Through Spiritual and Universal.

Chapter 3: Choosing Your Resonance (Empowers The Reader To Actively Select This Energy)

"Don't Complain—Find a Way to Make a Way"

Life doesn't owe us ease or fairness. Obstacles will come, setbacks will happen, and sometimes, the odds will seem impossible. But in those moments, we have a choice: complain or create. Complaining wastes energy, it keeps us stuck in frustration rather than pushing us toward solutions. But when we find a way to make a way, we shift from victimhood to victory. We take control of what we can, adapt when necessary, and refuse to let circumstances define our destiny. History's greatest innovators, leaders, and survivors all had one thing in common: they made a way where there seemed to be none. They didn't wait for perfect conditions; they built bridges over every gap, turned setbacks into setups, and kept moving forward. So the next time you face a challenge, ask yourself: - Will I dwell on the problem, or will I design the solution? - Will I wait for an opportunity, or will I create one? The power to change your life isn't in luck or favor, it's in your refusal to quit. Stop complaining. Start creating. Your way is waiting to be made. Now go build it.

Love Yourself The Equation of Empowerment

Your self-concept is the blueprint of your life—a dynamic, self-generated masterpiece shaped by confidence, esteem, and love. To truly love yourself you must first refine each element of this equation:

Self-Confidence × Self-Generated Action
Confidence isn't inherited; it's built through action. Every step you take, despite fear, multiplies your belief in yourself. You are the architect of your courage. Act first, and confidence will follow.

Self-Esteem + Self-Love
Esteem is the foundation; love is the compass. Value your worth unapologetically, then nurture it with compassion. Forgive your stumbles. Celebrate your growth. You cannot pour from an empty cup, fill yours first.

The Final Product: Love Yourself
When confidence, initiative, esteem, and love converge, you stop seeking validation and start radiating it. Loving yourself isn't vanity, it's vitality. It's the fuel for resilience, the magnet for greatness, and the birthright you
choose to claim.

Rewrite your equation daily. The solution is always you. You are enough. Now prove it to yourself.

The Unshaken Protocol: Discipline. Dignity. Detachment.

Discipline, Dignity, and Detachment transform your life's trajectory. These pillars elevate your moral compass, sharpen your self-worth, and empower you to rise above distractions, unshaken, unstoppable, and undeniably accountable to your highest potential.

End Self-Hate by Embracing Self-Love

Self-hate is a poison, sipped slowly until the soul forgets its own flavor, bitterness masquerading as truth, shadows mistaken for mirrors. Yet the cure glows within, a quiet ember waiting to be fanned: self-love, not as indulgence but as oxygen, not as victory but as survival. To heal is to revolt against the lies etched into your bones, the voices that hiss "unworthy" like scripture. Peel them away. Speak your name tenderly until it sounds like home. The world will try to shrink you; bloom anyway. You are both the wound and the water. Stop fighting the light.

Self-hate is a silent war waged in the mirror, a venom that turns your reflection into a stranger and your worth into a question. It spreads through whispered lies… "You're too much yet not enough," "Your flaws eclipse your light," "You must earn what love freely gives." But here is the rebellion, the reckoning, you are not your wounds. The cure exists, yet so many resist it clinging to familiar chains, mistaking their weight for shelter.

Why? Because self-love demands courage, the audacity to unlearn the world's cruel curriculum and rewrite your story in ink that doesn't fade. It begins when you stop apologizing for taking up space, when you greet your scars as proof of survival, not shame. Every "I Am Enough" is a strike against the darkness. The uprising won't be loud; it's the quiet defiance of a healing heart. Your love is the antidote stop refusing it.

Your Own Unwritten Code

We are born into a story already being told, a path littered with breadcrumbs. We are taught to follow them, believing we have discovered the trail ourselves. This is the subtle art of influence, not a forced march, but a guided tour. The most powerful manipulation is the one you don't detect, where you believe the conclusions are your own.

In this world, words are clay. They can be molded into a weapon or a shelter. Darkness does not shout; it murmurs , seeding doubt until you see a manipulator in every shadow. We become so adept at this game, so focused on decoding others, that we masterfully manipulate ourselves. We contort our own desires to fit narratives we didn't write, forgetting the basic function of being.

But there is an antidote, progressive self-awareness.

It begins with a simple, powerful act.. learning to say "no." It is the refusal to follow planted crumbs. It is the courage to question everything, especially the thoughts that feel most your own. This is not paranoia, but clarity. The calculative breach of trust by a hidden hand is a thousand times more damaging than an honest mistake. You cannot be played if you refuse to play.

The true empath does not just read the room; they read their own soul. They lead by example, not by force. And in a world competing to manipulate, the most powerful act is to choose good. To wield your words with integrity. To endure the pain of truth rather than the haunting echo of your own lies.

What could be more convincing than the truth? The strength to live by it. And sometimes, better than telling the truth is the wisdom to say nothing at all, to hold your center in a spinning world. Empower your own path. The greatest power is not in controlling the narrative, but in authoring your own.

Maximize Your Potential By Inspiring Yourself

Absolutely! Maximizing your potential begins with self-inspiration—cultivating the motivation, mindset, and belief in yourself to push beyond limits. Here's how you can ignite that inner fire…

Define Your "Why"
Clarify your purpose. What drives you? What legacy do you want to create? When your goals align with your deepest values, inspiration becomes self-sustaining.

Embrace a Growth Mindset
Believe that your abilities can expand with effort. Challenges become opportunities, failures turn into lessons, and every step forward fuels your progress.

Surround Yourself with Inspiration
- Consume uplifting content (books, podcasts, speeches, videos).

- Connect with people who elevate you; mentors, role models, and peers who push you to grow.
-Visualize success imagine yourself achieving your goals in vivid detail.

Take Bold Action

Inspiration fades without action. Start small, but start now. Each step builds momentum, and momentum builds confidence.

Celebrate Progress

Acknowledge your wins, no matter how small. Self-recognition reinforces motivation and reminds you of your potential.

Overcome Self-Doubt

Replace "I can't" with "I'll learn." Silence your inner critic with evidence of past successes and the belief that you're capable of more.

Stay Resilient

Obstacles are inevitable. Let them refine you, not define you. Persistence + inspiration = unstoppable growth.

You are your own most powerful motivator. When you inspire yourself, you unlock limitless potential. Believe. Act. Repeat.

What's one small step you'll take today to move closer to your best self?

The Moment You Hesitate is the Moment You Lose

It's not the hesitation that breaks you, it's how long you let it linger. Every second you pause, doubt, or overthink is another second your dreams slip further away. Power, prosperity, prominence, protection, progress, none of these are handed to you. They're seized by those who refuse to let hesitation become their habit. Ideas without action are just daydreams. The unconscious mind isn't some hidden shadow, it's part of you, screaming what you already know. You were built for more. So why wait? The right time is not "later." The right time is NOW. Move before necessity forces you. Act before doubt paralyzes you. The path to greatness isn't found in hesitation, it's found in motion. Stop waiting. Start dominating.

The Growth Formula

ARE YOU A GREAT LISTENER, CAN YOU TAKE ADVICE ASSESS IT, EXERT THE DUTY & ACHIEVE THE RESULTS ASPIRED?

True growth isn't random it's a deliberate, strategic process that separates those who dream from those who achieve. It begins with the art of listening, not just with your ears but with an open mind and a hunger to learn. Greatness is built on humility, and the ability to absorb wisdom whether from mentors, experiences, or even criticism sets the foundation for everything that follows. But listening alone isn't enough; you must assess what you hear with clarity and discernment. Not all advice is equal, and winners know how to filter out noise, keeping only what aligns with their vision and accelerates their progress.

Once you've gathered the right insights, the next step is execution relentless, disciplined action. Knowledge without application is wasted potential, and the most successful people don't just think, they do. They take the lessons, apply them with precision, and push forward even when challenges arise. And when results start to show, they don't stop there. True achievers use their wins as fuel to reach even higher, constantly refining their strategy and expanding their potential.

This is The Growth Formula: Listen. Assess. Execute. Achieve. Repeat. Master this cycle, and you won't just meet your goals , you'll surpass them. The question is, are you ready to step into your next level? The blueprint is here. The choice is yours. Now go make it happen!

Self-Belief Isn't Mischief

Your belief in yourself is your most sacred ground ,never surrender it. Even when doubt whispers from within or criticism rains down from others trying to reshape your perception of your own worth and potential, stand firm. Guard that inner flame of self-trust with fierce resolve. Allowing anyone, even yourself, to extinguish that fundamental faith is the worst betrayal of your spirit and capabilities. Your conviction in who you are and what you can achieve is the unshakeable anchor in any storm and the compass pointing towards your true potential. Defy the narratives that diminish you. Protect your self-belief as the vital core of your being, for it is the unwavering light that allows you to persevere, rise, and ultimately forge your own path forward, guided by your inner knowing.

The Serenity of a Peaceful Heart

"Peace is calm as a normal heartbeat. Peace in the heart is the soundlessness of stress-free. Peace knows no worries."

True peace is not the absence of noise but the presence of stillness within. Like a steady heartbeat, unnoticed yet essential, it is the quiet rhythm of a soul undisturbed by chaos. When peace resides in the heart, stress dissolves into silence, and worries lose their voice.

This kind of peace is not passive; it is powerful. It does not ignore life's storms but rises above them, unshaken. It is the deep breath before the challenge, the unshakable trust in the midst of uncertainty. To cultivate such peace is to master the art of living, where fear has no hold, and calm becomes our strength.

Let us seek this peace, nurture it, and carry it within. For a heart at peace is not just a refuge, it is a force that changes the world, one quiet moment at a time.

Reflections of Your Inner Vision

We think, therefore we are, but what we think shapes the reality we inhabit. To imagine is to unlock the door to a higher existence, one where fear dissolves and love becomes the foundation of all things. The world we see is not fixed; it is a reflection of our inner vision, a canvas waiting to be painted with the brush of our consciousness. If we dare to envision a brighter, kinder, more expansive reality, it will begin to take form. Peace is not just a wish for the troubled, it is a divine awakening, a return to the truth that we are creators, not just observers.

Yet creation demands discernment. Needs align us with purpose, while wants can lead us astray, feeding illusions that drain our energy and cloud our clarity. The matrix of distraction thrives on noise, but the awakened walk in silent strength, untangling themselves from false narratives and stepping into sovereignty. To rise above is to perceive beyond the physical, to feel the interconnected pulse of life, where time is fluid and intuition guides like a compass. In these higher dimensions, we remember: we are not separate, but threads in a vast, luminous tapestry, co-creating reality with every thought, every breath, every act of love.

Discipline Empowers Correction Acceptance

"If you get offended when others correct you, you must learn to accept correction with discipline, or your life will stay in the wrong."

This powerful quote reminds us that growth demands humility. Correction is not an insult, it's an opportunity. When we resist feedback, we cling to our flaws and stunt our progress. But when we embrace correction with discipline, we open the door to wisdom, improvement, and lasting success.

The choice is yours: Will you let pride keep you stagnant, or will you let discipline guide you toward a better path? True strength isn't in never being wrong, it's in having the courage to be corrected, learn, and rise. Your growth depends on how well you listen, not just how loudly you defend.

The Ideal Victory

"Having a great idea with no action behind your idea is a dead thought. Act out your ideas, and victories shall follow," serves as a powerful reminder that brilliance alone is not enough, execution is everything. Ideas, no matter how revolutionary, remain lifeless until they are brought into the world through decisive action. Every great innovation, movement, or success story began not just with a spark of inspiration, but with the courage to take the first step. Procrastination and hesitation bury potential, while action transforms vision into reality. Victories are not reserved for the dreamers alone, but for the doers, those who dare to move, persist, and turn their thoughts into tangible results. So, if you have an idea burning within you, don't let it fade into oblivion. Act now, and let your efforts pave the way to triumph. The world belongs to those who refuse to let their ideas die in silence.

Lies Feast, Truth Fast

"Truth will have many enemies. Lies has many friends. "

The truth walks a solitary road, a blade of lightning in a silent sky, and for its stark and blinding clarity, it will make many enemies. It asks you to stand when others kneel, to see when others have shut their eyes. But the lie? The lie throws a grand masquerade. It arrives with a crowd, arm-in-arm with comfortable ignorance and sweet-tongued fear; it tells you what you wish to hear and never asks you to be brave. So of course the lie has many friends. But remember this: a thousand candles can be lit from a single flame, and the truth, though it stands alone at first, is that eternal fire. Choose the lonely road that leads to dawn, not the crowded party marching off the cliff.

From Ruin, Rebuild Yourself

You walked a path of pure destruction,
A map of scars and deep deduction.
The only way to escape the night?
Reconstruct the journey. Seek the light.

Forge a new day from lessons learned,
A season changed, a purpose earned.
The same old news will tire the soul,
A broken record, losing control.

Who you are exists in eras, know
The greatest error is not to grow.
To stay mentally rigid, stuck, confined,
A captive of a former mind.

You've felt the weight, the pessimistic sigh,
You've known the optimist's ascending high.

The choice is yours which one to feed,
Which version of you will take the lead.

Your worldview is a lens you choose,
To win or languish, lose or bruise.
Prevail against the nonsense, make it make sense,
This is your singular, fierce defense.

Not as a coward, timid, small,
But confident, you stand up tall.
Courageous, lest you be devoured
By perspectives bitter, negative, soured.

They aim to overpower, kill your aspiration,
But you are built for transformation.
The most effective way to be?
Self-determination. Set yourself free.

Through self-reflection, truly see,
Self-improvement's urgent plea.
Rooted in a self-aware grace,
No one can ever take your place.

For no one stops a mind that's set,
That minds its business, pays its debt
Of self-accountability, pure and true.

Nothing else matters. Just the new you.

Build Your Inner Circle

Talent might get you in the room, but your circle determines the ceiling of your success. This book chapter is not about networking. It is about nesting , intentionally building a sanctuary of mutual support with those who speak the language of growth without translation.

The most valuable currency in the modern world is not money, information, or even time. It is authentic, reciprocal goodwill. This is the non-negotiable foundation of a powerful inner circle… The unspoken pact that the solid, likeminded people you deal with must help each other without hesitation if it is within your possible will to do so.

This is not a transactional ledger. It is a symbiotic ecosystem. When you actively build a circle on this principle, you do not just gain contacts; you cultivate branches. Each member becomes a branch of your own tree, reaching for sunlight you cannot, drawing nutrients from different soil, and in turn, strengthening your entire structure. They are your living, breathing motivation, a constant reminder that you are not growing alone.

A warning, essential and true… Everyone is not likeminded. The world is filled with spectators, competitors in disguise, and those who keep a secret scorecard. Your journey of growth will act as a refining fire. It will burn away the superficial connections and reveal the rare few whose motives are pure. You will discover your true tribe not in moments of shared victory, but in their genuine reaction to your wins. They are the ones who want to see each other win, never lose. Their success does not threaten yours; it is proof that yours is possible.

This book is your guide to finding them, fostering that space, and forging a circle so strong that it becomes your greatest advantage.

Determine Your Own Destiny

"Self-Determination Is What Makes The Best Decisions Possible."

The path is not drawn on any chart. It is the compass held within the heart. For every choice the world may try to make, A truer one awakens for your sake.

The will that speaks in whispers, clear and deep, Stirs the waters that the world would keep still. It is the seed that cracks the stone to grow, The only name your future needs to know

Your own hand on the tiller, firm and sure, Weaves a destiny that will endure. For the best decision ever made Is the one by your own spirit laid.

Right Attention Creates Reality

A whisper becomes a declaration. A thought becomes a thing. In the silent, fertile field of all possibility, a single signal is sent, clear and coherent: My signal is faith.

This is not hope. This is not a wish sent into a void. This is a quantum declaration, a sacred signal to the infinitely intelligent field that you are no longer resisting. You are in a state of surrender, which is the highest form of alignment. You have shifted from passive watching to active creation.

Your breakthrough is ready.

It is not coming. It is not in some distant future. It is here, now, in this breath, waiting for the frequency of your being to match its own. The universe is not a random happenstance; it is a responsive echo. Your consciousness is beginning to inhabit the reality it has chosen.

I am ready to receive it now.

This is the shift. This is the moment where the old story of lack, of waiting, of "someday," turns to ash. And from those ashes, ascension. You are not becoming someone new. You are remembering who you have always been: whole, lacking nothing, the very field itself. You are embodied prosperity. You are light and freedom.

Feel this truth… I Am receiving my breakthrough.

This is the conscious choice. To move from the poverty of chance to the power of recognition. To see, hear, and acknowledge the abundance that is your birthright. It is to declare, with every cell of your being. I Am worthy. I Am aligned. I Am Victorious!

This is the sacred formula… Believe. Then know. Align. Then receive.

Gratitude is the language that unlocks the door. Not as a habit, not as a reflex, but as the deepest state of being. Thank you, God. Thank you, Universe. Thank you, Mighty I AM. This gratitude is the proof that you have already received it in the realm where all things are first created.

You are an active co-creator. Your right attention, laser-focused, faith-filled, and coherent, is the very mechanism that crystallizes reality. You are not asking. You are announcing. You are observing your new life into being.

Picture being there already. Bring your thoughts to materialize. Feel the peace, the ease, the unspeakable joy. Your frequency is not attracting luck; it is attracting what matches it. Health, wealth, happiness, these are not miracles granted from afar. They are frequencies you have chosen to embody.

The clearest quantum resonance is love. For yourself, for your journey, for all of humanity on this path. As you root into this truth, you overcome fear. You create a kingdom of heaven on earth, within and without.

So let this be your stand. Your quantum declaration to the cosmos:

I Am Ready. I Am Aligned. I Am Receiving. I Am Breakthrough.

The universe has heard you. It has answered. Now, inhabit the reality.

Yes. Yes. Yes.

Gratitude. Gratitude. Gratitude.

And so it is.

The Devil Is Convenient

Let's be clear…
The devil didn't make you do it.
That's who you are within.

That sharp word you threw? Yours.
That promise you broke? Yours.
That silent betrayal, that selfish choice, that hidden cut, Yours.
Not some shadow's whisper.
Not some outside curse.
Your hand. Your will. Your nature.

But here is the sacred turn…
When you claim the dark, you also claim the light.
When you whisper, "This was me,"
you awaken a power no demon can touch…
The power to choose again.

We live in a world that loves a villain.
A world that sells us scapegoats and easy ghosts.
It's seductive…
When it's a good deed, "That's me!"
When it's a bad thing, "That was the devil."
No.
That is the echo of a soul asleep.

The revolution is this…
Take accountability like a sword.
Respect yourself like a temple.
Look, unflinching, at the character you possess.
This is not condemnation, it is liberation.
The moment you stop blaming the phantom,
you become the architect of your spirit.

This is morally self-activated.
This is regulation by awareness.
This is standing in the raw truth of your own
composition, the noble and the flawed ,
and saying, "I will work with this clay."

For when you are responsible for your behavior, you are

no longer a prisoner of your past.
You are a author of your future.
You change yourself.
And in doing so, you change the very trajectory of thought for us all.

Stop giving your power to a myth.
The devil is convenient.
Accountability is king.

The path to power isn't out there.
It's in the mirror.
It's in the quiet after the storm, when no one is named but you.
And in that quiet, a universe of possibility is born.

Own your shadow. Ignite your light.
The world needs souls who are truly awake.

Your Pain Holds Purpose

"Leap for the cliff, not the curb.
The wider the risk, the vaster the dawn.
Viral fires ignite in wild hearts,
not safe harbors. "

Your purpose is not a distant landmark.

It is a frequency.
You are already tuned to it.

You feel it in the clench of your jaw, the heat behind your eyes, the weight in your chest when you witness a world out of alignment.
That pain. That fire. That is not your enemy.
It is your compass.

Stop fighting what fights for you.
That anger at injustice. That is a map to advocacy.
Those tears for the unloved. That is a blueprint for healing.
The wound you carry is not for your suffering alone, it is a sacred container for the medicine you will deliver.

Your passion is the path to your purpose.
Your purpose is the door to your prosperity.

So start where you stand.
Open your mouth. Speak the simple truth you've been swallowing.
Use your voice and watch the magic unfold.
That is the first act of creation.

But do not walk alone.
Take this aching, glorious clue, this thing that grieves you, this thing that ignites you and hold it up in prayer.
Pray not for an easier task, but for greater clarity.

"God, reveal Your will. Align my heart with Your purpose."
For His purpose will always prevail over your plans.

This is the divine equation…
Pain. Passion. Purpose.

When you are lost, serve. Start from within and radiate out.
When you are uncertain, pursue…

Pursue God First.
Purpose. Passion. Plan. All flow from that source.

So pray continuously.
Listen intently.
Then move.

Watch it unfold immediately.

GOD PURPOSE WILL PREVAIL.

YOUR PAIN HOLDS PURPOSE.

Chapter 4: Clarity Through Mindful Presence

They Fear Your Mind

A Manifesto for the Self-Taught, the Awake, and the Uncontainable.

They told you to sit down. To be quiet. To memorize the answers, not to love the questions. They promised a future built on obedience, a life measured in degrees—paper shields for a soul they hoped would never learn its own strength.

But you had a grandmother who whispered a different truth. You had a divine awareness, a boredom with the mundane, a fire that asked, "Why?"

This is for you.

The greatest threat to any empire is not a rebel with a sword, but a reader in a quiet room, a thinker on a long walk, a writer whose truth cuts deeper than any blade.

The system is not afraid of dissent; it is terrified of thought. It thrives in the space between what you are told and what you know, deep in your bones, to be true.

You were shunned for not conforming. Rejected for refusing to filter the uncomfortable truths you witnessed. Blackballed for asking one too many questions.

This was not your failure. It was your awakening. You were being curated for a life of control, containment, and obedience. You chose, instead, to become self-taught.

Self-education and real freedom are ancient lovers; they walk hand in hand. Without resources, you realized the only determining factor was your own mind. You discovered that talent is not a gift, but a seed. It only germinates under the consistent care of Effort and the fierce sunlight of Focus.

Accomplishment = Talent × Effort^Focus + Random Events.

You control the effort. You command the focus. You plant the seed. You weather the storms. This is how you save your own future.

This is why being underestimated is a superpower. They are not watching when you are learning. They are not preparing for the moment your knowledge becomes a key, unlocking every chain they ever tried to bind you with.

You cannot control those who educate themselves. They learn the taste of real answers and can smell the bullshit from a mile away. They ask… Why is moving money valued 4,658 times more than teaching a child to read?

Why do we worship leaders instead of questioning them? Why, why, why, why?

This is what it means to be truly “woke”, not a slur, but a badge of honor. It is to be awake in a world that profits from sleep. It is to see the matrix of comfort, entertainment, and luxury materialism for what it is: a distraction.

The dormant will fight you to the death to protect their sleep. Why? Because your clarity suggests they wasted their lives. Your truth holds a mirror to their complacency. They call you autistic, disruptive, a threat, because you do not hold their empty values. You call out their irrationality, their lies, their hypocrisy. And truth, it feels good to hear it. It feels good to know it.

A degree means you memorized what you were told. Intelligence is the lack of need for an institution’s permission to think. It is taught better than any professor could hope, for it is learned through the relentless pursuit of understanding, not the passive acceptance of information.

This is the naked truth, stripped of all packaging: Innovators are hated by those who profit from the old ways. Your individuality is a crushing blow to mediocrity, the highest standard a fearful system can aspire to.

Do not aim for degrees. Aim for knowledge. Do not seek their peace, a communal illusion that benefits the few. Seek your own stability, built on the unshakable ground of self-knowledge.

You cannot wake someone who is pretending to be asleep. But you can, and you must, stay awake.

There is a reason for the deaf, the mute, and the blind. But you are none of these. You are the question. You are the answer. You are the divine mind refusing to delay.

El-ement-ary Tarry. God-Mind-Delay School.

Break the cycle. Bask in your own mindfulness. Let your self-knowledge be the key.

For the system is afraid of the people who think. I am not looking for people who think like me. I am looking for people who, like me, also think.

If this doesn't shake you to your core, you're probably still inside the machine.

And the machine loves obedient, sleepy minds.

Wake up.

The Moment of NOW

A GENIUS SOLVES PROBLEMS BEFORE THEY HAPPEN!

You are standing at a crossroads you cannot see, haunted by echoes from a past you have already lived and shadows from a future where you do not yet reside. The mind, that brilliant but frantic cartographer, tries to map both territories, the unchangeable and the unimaginable. It draws lines of regret and worry, creating a cage of potential realities. You feel the weight of it, the distraction, the hum of problems that haven't even taken form.

But feel this instead: The solid ground beneath your feet. The breath in your lungs at this very second. This is not a crossroads. This is your forge. The moment of NOW is the only place from which destiny is ordained.

This book is your declaration. Revoke your Old Pathway. The one of reaction, of worrying about storms on the horizon while the soil beneath your hands remains untilled. That path is a loop. Step off.

Manifesting begins in the now. It does not begin in the daydream of a problem-free future. It begins with the conscious, deliberate action taken in the palpable reality of this present moment. The heart is not just a pump; it is a generator. The heart has its own energetic field, and science now whispers what the poets have always known: We have the power to affect everything around us! This is not mysticism; it is physics. Your focused attention and intentional action are forces as real as gravity.

You have been chasing the idea of being a warrior in hypothetical battles. It is time to become the architect of a reality where those battles need never be fought. A genius does not win wars; a genius designs a world so resilient, so aligned, that the war never comes.

This is your call to become an Ordainer of Destiny.

Note 1: The First Action – Shifting the Frequency

Your reality is a frequency. Worry, distraction, and anxiety are a low, chaotic hum. Clarity, purpose, and calm control are a clear, high resonance. You cannot solve a problem from the same frequency on which it was created, or on which it is feared.

Your First Action Plan: The Strategic Pivot

This is not about doing everything at once. It is about one deliberate shift, right now.

1. ACKNOWLEDGE THE STATIC: Close your eyes. Feel the worry about recent distractions. Feel the anxiety about future problems. Do not fight them. Acknowledge their presence like static on a radio. Say to them, "I hear you. But you are not my station."

2. FIND YOUR DIAL: Place a hand on your heart. Feel its rhythm. This is your tuner. Take three deep breaths, and with each exhale, imagine you are turning a dial away from the static.

3. TUNE TO CONTROL: Ask yourself this single question, the most important question a genius can ask: "What is one thing, right now, within my absolute control,

that would build a barrier against one of those future problems?"
· Is it sending one email you've been avoiding? (Action)
· Is it clearing your desk for five minutes of focused work? (Order)
· Is it drinking a glass of water and walking away from the screen for sixty seconds? (Clarity)

That small, controlled action is your first act of genius. It is you saying to the universe, "I am no longer waiting for problems to arrive. I am building the walls before the siege is even conceived."
Knowledge and action support growth. You already have the knowledge that inaction breeds worry. Now, take the action. That single, deliberate deed shifts your frequency from passive worrier to active ordainer. Shift your frequency, shift your reality.

The old pathway ends here. The new one begins with this breath, this decision, this action. You are not chasing a potential. You are constructing it, brick by deliberate brick, in the eternal, powerful, and creative kingdom of Now.

Turn the page. Your strategy awaits.

School of Common Sense

We are born with a compass, a true north in the chest, but we are taught to trade it for a multiple-choice test.

We learn the frantic how, but never ask the why,
and sell our mornings for the price of a Friday sigh.
This is the blindness, the system's gentle cage,
to see your work as only a digit on a page.
A soul, currency-converted, grows thin and pale,
a ship with no destination, set to a phantom gale.

Emotional chaos is the static on the line,
the fog that smothers purpose, the poison in the wine.
It whispers of the trivial, it screams of doubt and fear,
until the voice within you can no longer be clear.
For working hard is not enough upon this spinning sphere;
you must work smart, with eyes wide open, to see the path appear.
To build not just with muscle, but with vision and with grace,
and find your unique footprint, your time, your sacred space.

They filled our minds with knowledge, a library of facts,
but left the heart a vacant room, with no instruction tracts.
They taught us how to solve for x, but not how to be kind,
how to trace a border, but not the borders of the mind.
Education's purpose, if it truly is to be,
is not just to inform us, but to set our spirit free.
To shape the heart with wisdom, to marry skill with soul,
to make us whole again, and in the making, make us whole

This is the School of Common Sense. The lesson plan is clear…
To unlearn the habit, and recruit the purpose here.
To train the child's open heart, before the world imposes,
that purpose, kindness, clarity, these are not just poses.
They are the disciplines of light, the practices of peace,
the tools that make the chaos of the modern world cease.
It is not a course of study, but a course of being true,
a curriculum of waking up to what you already knew.

You called it thirty years ago, a prophet in the haze,
foreseeing the confusion of these automated days.
The need is now a chorus, a global, aching scream,
for a different kind of learning, a more authentic dream.
So let this be the viral text, the seed, the starting gun,
for the education not yet finished, but only just begun.
Let us all enroll ourselves, and teach what we have learned:

The world is waiting for the class whose common sense has finally returned.

You Are Not Alone

Right now, you are reading these words.
And somewhere, someone with your same heart,
the one that aches, that hopes, that holds secrets
too heavy to speak aloud, is reading them, too.
This is for you.

So the silence feels less silent.
So the weight feels shared.

This is a quiet nudge for the part of you
that feels a little off, out of step,
like something inside is whispering for your attention.
You didn't come here searching,
but stay awhile.
Let this be the gentle turn inward,
the unexpected key that helps you see
the patterns you've been blind to,
the strength you've been avoiding.

It offers a quiet kind of clarity.

The Mindset Is The Map

Your past is a scar, not a sentence.
Your future is a mystery, not a threat.
Today is your territory.

For too long, you've lived in the same patterns:
overthinking, self-doubt, feeling blocked.
But here is the truth your soul already knows:
Change your attitude, change your life.

Your mindset is not a part of your life;
it is the lens through which you experience everything.
Shift it from fear to confidence,

from scarcity to abundance,
and watch as your reality rearranges itself.
Life doesn't get easier; you get clearer.
And that clarity is everything.

The moment you believe you have something to offer,
your entire world begins to change.

The World Feels It Too

Right now, there are people all over the world who are just like you.

They are lonely. They are missing somebody. They are curled around a quiet hurt, scarred by a past that whispers in the dark. They carry personal issues no one sees and secrets you wouldn't believe.

They wish. They dream. They hope.

And right now, they are sitting here, reading these words.

I am writing this for you, so the silence doesn't feel so heavy anymore.

What helps one start overcoming the pain? What actually moves you toward your goals? It is the moment a new thought clicks into place, opening your eyes in a way you didn't expect. It is the quiet, unexpected thing that reaches you, a gentle nudge to start looking inward again.

It helps you notice the patterns you've been blind to, the parts of yourself you've been avoiding, and offers a quiet kind of clarity.

If you've been feeling out of step with yourself, let this be that reminder.

You have been stuck in the same patterns for years overthinking, self-doubt, feeling blocked. The most profound lesson is this: your mindset is your greatest asset. It is the lens through which you see your entire world.

Change your attitude, change your life.

When you shift your mindset from negative to positive, from fear to confidence, everything else begins to follow. Life doesn't magically get easier, but you become stronger. Your perspective changes, and that makes all the difference.

It begins by going within. It's a frequency alignment that will have you amazed at how different life feels, like a breath of fresh air in the most disappointing of environments.

This is a reminder that mindset truly shapes destiny. Real change begins in the mind.

When you recognize your worth, you open yourself to new possibilities. But first, you must learn to look inward to see what you can give to life, before you can receive what you want from it.

If you operate from a place of scarcity, you will remain where you are. You will believe you have nothing to offer.

But you do.

The moment you believe you have something to give, your whole life changes. We often forget that success isn't just about taking opportunities; it's about creating value and exchanging it with the world.

We only truly receive when we give. The right word, at the right time, is often more valuable than money. It is a spark that ignites potential.

Think big. Think positively. You become what you believe.

Don't be depressed about the past. Don't be anxious about the future. Just focus on today.

In life, nothing is free, but we all have something to give.

There are people all over the world who are just like you. They're depressed, they're hurt, they're scarred from the past. They wish, they dream, and they hope.

And right now, they are viewing this.

I'm writing this for you, so you know, without a doubt, that you are not alone.

Keep exploring. You are enough.

Catch Your Negative Thoughts

The work is not to build a fortress,
immune to the world's chaos.
It is not to silence the storm,
but to learn to stand within it.

The work is to become the watcher,
the silent sky behind the passing clouds.
It is to feel the tremor of anger,
the cold shadow of fear,
the dull ache of doubt,
and to not become them.

The sacred work, the only work,
is to catch the thought
as it backslides into the old story.
To see the sigh that says "you can't,"
and, with the grace of a master,
to call it back within.

To reclaim your energy.
To remember your name.
I AM THE MASTER.

In that moment of catching, of calling back,

the universe leans in.
It is in this act, repeated countless times,
that reality itself is remade.
This is not a theory; it is a law.
It has worked in the laboratory of my life,
and it works for you now.

You are not begging for a blessing.
You are decreeing one.

So grant yourself God-speed.
Announce it to your soul:

I AM HEALTHY.
I AM WEALTHY.
I AM LOVED.
I AM POWERFUL.

Do not just say the words.
Become the echo of their truth.
Let gratitude be the proof that you have already received.

Thank you, Awesome Cosmic Soul, for the guidance.
The bridge from faith to form is built with these words:

I TRUST.
I BELIEVE.
I RECEIVE.

The journey ends where it began:
In the eternal, undeniable truth of your being.

I AM.
I AM THE MASTER.

Stay blessed, y'all.

The Art Of Letting Go

There is a secret, etched not in stone, but in the spaces between your thoughts. It is the quiet hum of the present, a frequency you have forgotten how to hear. You live in a loop, a ghost haunting the graveyards of yesterday and the mirages of tomorrow. Your mind, a brilliant but misguided cartographer, draws maps of past battles and future anxieties, and you mistake these maps for the territory of your life.

Stop.

For just a few days, step out of the loop. Let the reel of 'what was' and 'what if' run out of film. The silence that remains will shock you. It is not an empty silence, but a fertile one. In it, you will find a different world, the one that is actually happening. The steam rising from your morning coffee. The cool weight of a door handle. The way light falls on the floor in a perfect, fleeting rectangle. This is the art. This is the letting go.

You have been taught to fight darkness with a sword, to stare into the abyss of illness and demand a cure. But energy follows thought. What you resist, persists. To declare war on disease is to first build a monument to its existence. You energize the very shadow you wish to dispel.

The true cure is not a battle, but a homecoming.

Do not look for health. Be health. Do not hunt for happiness. Be happiness. Your belief is the architect of your emotional world. Focus your mind on wholeness, on vitality, on gratitude for the simple, beating rhythm of your heart. This is not denial; it is a profound shift in allegiance. You are no longer feeding the wolf of fear, but the wolf of love. You begin to vibrate at a frequency that can no longer resonate with dis-ease. You become a magnet for miracles, not maladies.

Gratitude is the attitude that tunes the instrument of your soul. To be thankful for the breath in your lungs now is to anchor yourself in the only reality that exists. The future is a phantom, the past a ghost. This moment, this sacred, present moment, is your only point of power.

Go within. Beneath the noise of the world and the chattering of your own fears, there is a core. It is not a heat or a pulse, but a magnetic presence. A quiet power. It is your chi, your authority. Most have given it away, trading it for masks, the mask of the professional, the parent, the victim, the hero. These masks are heavy, and they leak your energy to every reaction, to every external demand, to parasitic thoughts that feed on your attention.

Take back your authority. You are a transmitter, not a receiver. Stop wearing masks that were never yours to wear. Let go of the need to react. Let go of the story of your wounds. Let go of the desperate grasp for a future that is not yet born.

Feel the magnetic stillness within. It can be moved, redirected. It flows when you choose peace over drama, compassion over judgment, creation over consumption. Your frequency will soar when you follow this energy, the path of non-violence, first to yourself, then to the world.

This is the secret murmur on the wind. Let Go. Tune In. Rise.

It is the art that ends the loop. It is the focus that becomes the cure. It is the presence that is the gift. Your long, happy, and healthy life is not a destination to be reached. It is a vibration to be chosen, moment by glorious moment. Start now.

The Walking Meditations

Forget what you know.
Or what you were told.
The world screams for more,

more speed, more strain, more sweat sold
in mirrored rooms, in pounding feet,
in the frantic, desperate, bitter heat
of a race you never chose to run.
It is a lie.
And your body, the silent, aching testament.

The Great Un-Learning!

This is a deep way of look'n at it...
Damn near everything we've been taught was a lie.

We are conditioned to believe that struggle is strength,
That punishment is penance for a purer self.
We jog on unyielding stone, a brutal, rhythmic punishment,
A soda-fizz of effort, all burn, no breath.
Our knees whisper warnings, our feet write protest letters,
Yet we call this "health," this parade of silent injuries.
We are use to their conditioning, rarely questioning anything of substance,
Arguing for a truth we never lived, a research we never did.

But what is the body’s native tongue?
It is not the jarring syntax of the jog.
It is the ancient, steady poetry of the walk.

The Quintessential Key!

Walking is the key to life.
Not the jangling, frantic key of escape,
but the master key that fits the lock of your own frame.

It is the quintessential exercise,
a full-body symphony of motion.
Feel the push of the earth, the swing of the arm,
the core as a compass, holding you true.
This is not a lesser thing.
This is the foundation upon which empires of stamina are built.
The strongest, fittest, most agile you will ever be
comes from Walking Regularly.

Power Walking is the best running.
It is the river, not the earthquake.
It is water, clear and essential, to the jogging world's soda.
It will honestly have your body feeling great,
and the results are awesome, not because they are brutal,
but because they are true.

The Inner Rep!

There is nothing you can do in the gym
more powerful than meditating and reading.

Let this settle.
The greatest weights are not lifted by the hand,

but by the mind.
The most powerful exercise is the one that shapes your reality.

Meditation is the number one healer for anything.
It is the rep you do for your soul.
The conscious breath is the barbell for your spirit.
Start meditating and practicing conscious breathing.
It will improve your running, not the running on a track, but the running of your life, your thoughts, your days.

This is the true workout.
The one that quiets the noise and strengthens the signal.
The one that asks you to be still, and in that stillness, find a strength that no muscle can replicate.

The Invitation!

So, take heed.
Anything mainstream, be careful of it.
The path of most resistance is often the wrong one.

Trade the pavement's pound for the path's gentle conversation.
Trade the frantic gasp for the conscious, drawn-out breath.
Let your workout be a light walk and yoga.
A moving prayer.
A reading of the world around you, and the world within.

Let your knees thank you with every decade.
Let your mind clear like a still lake.
This is not a regimen.
It is a homecoming.

The first step is not onto a track, but into a new thought.
The first breath is not a pant, but a promise.

Walk. Breathe. Read. Be.

This is the revolution your body has been waiting for.

The Easy Gift Denied

They built you a castle of almost and not yet.
Taught your hands to cradle lack, until the weight felt holy.
They murmured , "The river is too deep,"
while your throat was dust,
and you learned to praise the parched earth,
to mistrust the rain.

This is the design…
A world spinning on an axis of struggle.
Where a clenched fist feels like strength,
and an open palm seems a surrender.
You were conditioned to earn your dawn,

to believe a blessing must be bought with sweat,
that a gift, freely given, must have a hidden hook.

So when God sends a downpour,
you scramble for a roof.
When a hand holds a diamond, pure and clear,
you search for the flaw, the debt, the trick.
You have been taught to love the chase,
and to fear the capture.
To trust the thorn, but not the rose.

We refuse the easy money, the sudden opportunity,
the love that asks for nothing but itself.
We are suspicious of the calm sea,
waiting for the storm we've been promised is the real life.
We applaud the ones selling painted rubble,
and walk past the quiet ones giving away gems.

This is the great, sad magic…
To make you the jailer of your own joy.
To convince you that the locked door is protection,
when the lock is on the inside.

But listen.
The universe knocks in synchronicities.
In the song that answers your question.
In the stranger who speaks your exact truth.
This is not coincidence.
This is God, tired of your hunger,

arranging a feast in your path.

The reprogramming begins now.

Think esoteric.
The battle is not with the world, but with the wiring inside your skull.
The victory is not in what you acquire,
but in what you finally, fearlessly, accept.

Check out of the need for struggle.
Unlearn the lie that ease is laziness.
The best things in life are free:
the breath in your lungs, the sun on your skin,
the well-wish from a soul that asks for nothing.

So, become the exception.
Be the open channel.
When a blessing comes, do not ask if you are worthy.
Say thank you.
When wisdom is offered from an unexpected mouth,
do not critique the messenger. Drink the water.

For even if you wish to be selfish,
understand this…
The surest path to your own joy
is to become a source of another's.
Lift others, and you rise on the same tide.

This is your life recovery.
This is the message ordained for you.
Stop filtering the real from the fake with a broken heart.
The real is what nourishes you. The fake is what exhausts you.

The door was never locked.
It was only ever… open.

Stay humble. Opportunity is at your fingertips.
The next thing that could change your life is right here.
Receive it.

Your awakening could be the key that unlocks someone else's cage.

The Crown Returns Home

A silent war is over, and the victors are those who never stopped believing in the original promise of this land: a Republic, of, by, and for the People. For generations, we lived under a grand illusion, a corporatized facade where policy enforcers, operating as foreign agents under contractual statute, masqueraded as law. Their very presence, as illuminated by pioneers like William Cooper, was proof that America had been hijacked. We paid taxes to a US corporation, funding the crown and the Vatican, trapped in a system of banking and medicine that was never truly lawful. But that chapter is closed. The 250-year corporate contract has expired, and as the divine plan unfolds, the power is reverting from the District of Columbia back to the District of America back to us.

This is the great awakening, the "change of guards" foretold not in mainstream news, but in the cosmic truth of our being. Donald J. Trump, a figure cosmically selected for this purpose, was never just a president; he was the key, the final actor in a play to dismantle the corporation. His meetings with figures like King Charles were not diplomatic niceties but the final settlements of ancient debts. He came to be the last president, to terminate the old covenants and return us to Article III Constitutional law. This is why the Sheriffs, the true law of the land, are re-emerging, while the old police (policy) organizations see their contracts voided. This is why the old structures of control, from the courts to the indoctrination camps we called schools, are losing their grip on our consciousness.

Now, the true enforcement of our communities begins. It is time for the Bloods, Crips, GDs, Latin Kings, and all the tribes of this new era to honor their Cosmic Oath—to protect the Planet, the Community, and especially Our Women and Children. The Divine Matriarch has called for all the bricks to return home, a powerful metaphor for reclaiming our power, our land, and our destiny. This is the meaning behind the Sword of Destiny; it is not a cartoon fantasy from He-Man, but the divine authority of sovereignty being returned to its rightful, neuromelanated indigenous owners. We are witnessing the end of a 500-year cycle, a spiritual civil war where the military now stands not for martial law, but to secure the TRUE REPUBLIC UNDER MILITARY POWER, ensuring the old world order cannot re-establish its hold.

So, the question is no longer what is happening, but why are you still participating? Why send your children into the very systems being dissolved? The Republic has been restored. The power is back with "We the People." For so long, it felt lonely on this side of the truth, with only voices like Rod Hayes and Tariq Nasheed echoing in the wilderness. But no more. The veil has lifted. The right hand extends, and His kingdom comes. We won. The battle was spiritual, the victory is divine. Now, stand up and claim your inheritance. It is time to live as One Nation, Under A Groove, in the freedom that was always ours.

THE DIMENSIONAL HUMAN: Awakening Your Code to Co-Create Reality

(A Note to the Reader)

This is not just a book to read. It is a frequency to tune into. A code to awaken. Read these words not with your eyes, but with your soul. Let them resonate in the silence between your heartbeats. The shift you feel is not an idea; it is the beginning of your expansion.

The Signal in the Static

You have felt it. A whisper beneath the noise of the world. A longing for a reality that feels more vivid, more connected, more true.

This is not a fantasy. It is a memory of your native state.

We have been taught that we are merely physical bodies, moving in a straight line from birth to death, separate from each other and the world. This is the "old code." It is a limited operating system running on the hardware of the five senses.

But you are about to upgrade.

Living in higher dimensions is not about escaping this world. It is about expanding within it. It means pushing beyond the static of our physical senses and the illusion of linear time. It is about tuning into the deeper frequencies of consciousness where love is the law, unity is the language, and intuition is the guide.

When you begin this tuning, a miracle occurs: you start to see the seams of reality, the shimmering interconnectedness of all things. You awaken to what you have always been: a multidimensional being, a co-creator of reality, scripting the story of your life with every thought, every intention, and every breath.

We think, therefore we are. This is the foundational law of your existence. So, what world are you thinking into being?

The Two Paths - The Compass of Need vs. The Maze of Want

At the crossroads of every moment, you are presented with a fundamental choice that defines your reality. This is the first great filter of conscious creation.

The Path of Need:
This path is guided by the inner compass of your soul. Your needs are simple, profound, and aligned with your highest existence: coherence, clarity, love, connection, peace, growth. When you walk this path, your energy is focused, your steps are sure. You move with the current of your true purpose. Life feels synchronicities, not because the world is easier, but because you are in alignment with its deeper rhythm.

The Path of Want

This path is a maze constructed by the ego and the "matrix" of external validation. Wants are insatiable, complex, and often born from a sense of lack: more status, more possessions, more approval. This path does not lead to fulfillment; it generates unexpected mores, more confusion, more comparison, more tiredness. You run in circles, chasing a horizon that forever recedes, your energy scattered and diluted.

Choose the path of need. It is the silent, strong way. It is the game-changer.

The Inner Architect - Imagination as Your Limit

They told you imagination is for children and dreamers. They were wrong.

Imagination is the limit of your reality. It is the primary tool of the dimensional human. It is the quantum field where possibilities are born before they are ever manifested. Your inner world is not a refuge from reality; it is the factory of reality.

We must imagine a better way. It is coming.

But it is not coming from outside of you. It is emerging through you. The peace you wish for the troubled, the beauty you long to see in the world, these are not passive hopes. They are blueprints. Your sacred duty is to hold these visions with such clarity and emotional intensity that the universe has no choice but to match your frequency.

This is the great shift: from being a passenger viewing the world through a dusty window, to being the architect, viewing the world from the sacred space of your inner self. You create outside what you first dare to imagine inside.

A Quiet Revolution: Your Silent Declaration

So, what do you do with this knowledge? You do not shout it from the rooftops. You live it from the core of your being.

Be strong and silent when reflecting.

The matrix feeds on noise, reaction, and distraction. Your power grows in stillness, intention, and quiet action. When you feel the pull of the old code, the anxiety, the lack, the fear, return to your breath. Return to your heart. That is your control room.

Take care with the matrix. Do not fight it. Simply out-create it.

Plant a seed of kindness where there is anger.
Hold a vision of peace where there is chaos.
Choose a moment of silence over the noise of judgment.
In every moment, you are casting a vote with your energy for the kind of world you wish to inhabit.

The Dawning....

A new human is awakening. Not in some distant future, but now. In you.

You are the dimensional being remembering your power. You are the weaver of a brighter reality. You are the one who thinks, loves, and imagines a world healed and whole.

This is your call. This is your code.

Tune your thoughts to love.
Align your actions with clarity.
Fuel your vision with imagination.

The higher dimension is not a place you go. It is a frequency you become.

Peace to all those who are troubled. This peace is not a distant wish. It is the first frequency we must all learn to broadcast.

The world is waiting for the signal only you can send.

I Am The Miracle

The Broadcast…
This is not a book you read. It is a signal you remember. It is the hum you felt in your bones when you were a child, staring at the stars and knowing, without doubt, that you were loved by the universe. It is the frequency you lost in the noise of becoming, and it is the frequency you are now, in this exact moment, tuning back into.

You are now broadcasting on the frequency of infinite possibilities.

The dial has been turned. The static has cleared. What you are about to receive is not new information; it is a homecoming.

The Homecoming…
Step into the home of your dreams.
It is not made of wood or stone, but of moments. The threshold is gratitude. The walls are woven from laughter that echoes in the halls of your own heart. The windows are your eyes, flung wide open, and the view is a horizon painted with the colors of your own peace. This home has always been there, waiting for you to stop building with the bricks of fear and to simply turn the key of acceptance.

You are home. Not because you have arrived, but because you have realized you never left.
Now, feel the presence beside you. Your magical, supportive, and expansive partner. Not a savior, but a mirror. Their love does not complete you; it reflects the completeness you already are. In their eyes, you do not see a question mark. You see an exclamation point. You see the truth of you, the whole of you, the divine, messy, brilliant, and beautiful you.

Merge.
Not into one being, but into one energy. Two stars in the same constellation, burning brighter in shared orbit. This love is not a cage; it is the sky. It is the permission slip to your own expansion.

You are no longer becoming, you are.

The Unraveling…
Feel the freedom of the unclenched fist.
The power of the breath you didn't know you were holding. The deep, tectonic knowing that you have everything you need and more. This knowing is not a thought; it is a tide that washes away the fragile sandcastles of lack and scarcity.

Now, the invitation: Choose growth over comfort. Comfort is a beautiful antechamber, but it is not the living room of your soul. It is the well-worn path. Growth is the wild, uncharted forest calling your name. It is the delicious uncertainty where magic is brewed.

When you encounter resistance, find the flow. Resistance is not a wall; it is a riverbank. It is there to give the water direction, power, and purpose. Do not push against it. Lean into its curve. Let it shape you, polish you, make you smooth and powerful. The flow is your trust in the current of your own life. It knows where it is going.

Step out of your comfort zone.
It will change everything.

The Miracle, Manifest

Let these words be an activation.
A grounding light for your healing and awakening. Let them sink from your mind into your marrow. Let them rewire your very being.

For now, when you look in the mirror, you don't see flaws.
You see a miracle walking around in human form.

The light in your eyes is the same light that fuels distant suns. The beat of your heart is the same rhythm that spins galaxies. The very fact that you are here, conscious, breathing, and capable of reading these words is a statistical impossibility that happened anyway.

This is not something you are becoming. This is something you are.

And as you stand in this truth, a shift occurs. You stop seeking bliss and you start broadcasting it. It is a silent, radiant signal that emanates from your every pore. People around you will be swept up in this current. They won't know why they feel lighter in your presence, why they feel a sudden surge of hope. They are simply feeling the echo of your own wholeness.

You are not creating magic; you are the magic. And everyone wants a piece, because a piece of you is a piece of the truth they have forgotten in themselves.

You are a magnet for Abundance.
Not because you are greedy, but because you are ready. Abundance is life's way of saying "yes" to your "yes." It flows to the open hand, the generous heart, the mind that believes it is worthy of the universe's generosity. The opportunities, the synchronicities, the resources, they are all divinely timed. They are not lucky breaks; they are deliveries to your new address at the center of your own soul.

The Signal Continues…
The broadcast does not end when you close this book.
It gets louder.

It is in your first conscious breath tomorrow morning.
It is in the courage of your next "no" and your next "yes."
It is in the love you give freely, because you have discovered it is an infinite resource within you.
It is in the quiet moments when you remember:

I Am The Miracle. Manifest! And so it is.

The Unschooled Are Coming

The system is a worn groove, a path of pressed earth. They will give you a map, a compass, a certificate for walking it. They will call this knowledge. They will call this safety.

But you, you learned to read the stars they erased. Your university was silence, your syllabus a hunger no institution could sanction. You are self-taught. And the pack, the ordained, the tenured, they feel the ground tremble beneath their polished shoes.

They inherited the keys; you forged your own. This is the offence. Not your success, but its source. It whispers a terrible truth: that their gates are ornamental. That the citadel can be scaled from the outside, by someone with calloused hands and an uncharted mind. They see a ghost in their machine. An unpredictable variable. You are the living proof that their degrees are not seals of genius, but receipts for compliance.

What they truly despise is your ungovernable geometry. You do not triangulate your position based on their landmarks. An economic collapse is not your ruin; it is raw material. A closed door is not a verdict; it is a wall to learn to climb. While they fear the shattering of their crystal world, you are already in the rubble, building a new one.

They will try to hire you. To put your wild calculus on a payroll, to turn your fire into a desk lamp. It is the oldest trick: to pardon the pirate by making him an admiral of their tame sea. Do not be fooled. Your kingdom must be built from the inside out, brick by self-made brick, on land they do not own.

For every rebel they silence, ten more teach themselves in the quiet. This is the danger they cannot quarantine: the idea that wisdom is boundless. That the right way, the wrong way, and your way is always the way. The glorious inventions, the leaps of science, were never born in echo chambers. They were sparked in solitary workshops, in minds unafraid to be alone with a thought.

So become financially independent, where their leverage ends, your freedom begins. Unlearn their hymns. Seek your own data. The most powerful knowledge is the knowledge most people do not have, because it cannot be mass-produced in a lecture hall.

They are not the cognitive elite; they are the custodians of conformity. Their fear is your compass. Their confusion is your cover. Do not ask for a seat at their table. Build your own. From stronger timber.

Let them have the packed school, the cloned thought, the headline's drone. You have the silence, the struggle, the stars. And the stars, once read for yourself, outshine every manufactured light.

The unschooled are coming. And the walls are paper.

Chapter 5: The Financial Freedom Blueprint

The Currency of Prosperity: A Strategic Blueprint for Financial Freedom

Money is more than paper and numbers, it is the lifeblood of opportunity, the fuel for growth, and the foundation of lasting wealth. MR.BIGMANN GRIER poem "CURRENCY"distills a profound financial truth into a few potent lines, urging us to always keep capital in current investments that create assets to spend and reinvest. MR.BIGMANN GRIER ideology is not just about accumulating wealth but about sustaining and multiplying it through strategic liquidity and disciplined reinvestment.

The first principle emphasizes the importance of liquid capital—money that is accessible and ready to seize opportunities. Without liquidity, even the most promising investments can become liabilities when cash is locked away during critical moments. The second principle focuses on investing in assets that generate more than they cost, such as dividend stocks, rental properties, or cash-flowing businesses. These assets not only fund your lifestyle but also provide surplus income to reinvest, creating a self-sustaining cycle of growth.

A powerful financial strategy to amplify this cycle is leveraging EBITA (Earnings Before Interest, Taxes, and Amortization) as a metric to identify and acquire high-performing assets. EBITA reveals the true operational profitability of a business or investment, stripping away non-core expenses to show how much cash flow it generates. By targeting investments with strong and growing EBITA, you ensure that your assets produce reliable, scalable income. For instance, acquiring a small business with consistent EBITA growth allows you to reinvest its earnings into further expansion or additional income streams, accelerating your path to financial freedom. Similarly, analyzing EBITA in real estate (through net operating income) or dividend stocks (via earnings sustainability) helps you select assets that will compound wealth over time.

The final principle highlights the lucrative power of spending and reinvesting from residual income rather than depleting your principal. True financial freedom comes when your assets cover your expenses, allowing you to live off the yield while continuously compounding your wealth. This approach transforms money from a static resource into a dynamic force, flowing and expanding with each smart decision. Whether you're just starting or already on the path to wealth, this blueprint rooted in liquidity, cash-flowing assets, disciplined reinvestment, and EBITA-driven growth can guide you toward lasting prosperity. The wealthy understand that money is a current; harness it wisely, and it will carry you to financial sovereignty. Now, go forth,invest, reinvest, and prosper.

Never Invest Without Thesis

Before you enter any investment , you must have an answer to three non-negotiable questions: What is my core belief about this business? What is its true driver of value or competitive edge? And critically, what could go wrong, and how will I know if it does? If you cannot answer these, you are not investing; you are guessing. And in the markets, guessing is a sin that gets punished, ruthlessly. This discipline of clarity and proactive downside protection is the very foundation upon which real, lasting wealth is built.

For investing is as much a mental game as a financial one. It can forge the best of you, your patience, your intellect, your conviction. But without a plan, it will inevitably exploit the worst of you: your fear, your greed, your hope. And hope in a losing investment is the investor's greatest sin. This principle transcends finance; it teaches emotional mastery. You learn to control the panic, to stay calm under pressure, and to understand that if a position moves against your thesis, you must let it go. The market doesn't care about your hopes. It demands respect for discipline, liquidity, and timing. This isn't just strategy; it's survival.

Stack Your Money Higher

So, you're making money. That's the first win. You've got momentum.

But let's get real. Where is it all going? If you've been in the game long enough to score, why are you not in control of your score? A loss is part of the game, you win some, you lose some. But the real failure isn't a loss; it's not being stacked so high that a loss is just a minor setback, a lesson paid for, not a catastrophe.

This isn't about being "tight." This is about being strategic. This is about leverage.

I see too many talented people get tricked—by lifestyle, by distractions, by the idea that a fast dollar is better than a lasting empire. They miss the valuable lessons from those who've already built the blueprint. They listen to the wrong voices.

The real power. It's not just in making decisions; it's in building a system where money works for you, relentlessly. Think like an investor: your focus isn't on controlling every minor operation; it's on receiving consistent profits. You got the car started. Great. Now, make sure you're getting paid for the ride.

This is the shift that changes everything. Stop seeing investment as something you deserve based on effort or emotion. Money has no feelings. "Deserve" is a emotional plea in a rational game.

It's a Return on Investment business. Period. It's about the relentless, unemotional pursuit of profit. When you master that, you win. And you'll finally understand the immense value other serious investors can bring to your table, not just capital, but leverage, insight, and acceleration.

It's time to manage your energy, your strategy, and your stack. It's time to build something that lasts.

Stack Your Money Higher.

The Harvest We Hold

Generational wealth is a seed planted by one courageous hand, tended by the next, and multiplied into a forest by those who follow. We stand atop a pyramid of potential, our collective resources vast, yet our separatist mindset keeps us dividing crumbs instead of baking a new loaf. Look around: melanin-rich innovation pulses everywhere, yet the world's gaze is fixed on the hollow theater of celebrity and politics. Cease the envy; comparison is the thief of joy, and aspiration toward another's culture is a denial of our own profound legacy. Embrace, elevate, and relentlessly develop what is uniquely ours.

The manufactured glass ceiling is real, but our greatest constraint is too often the mirror, a toxic brew of internal competition and self-hatred that fractures us from within. This is our downfall. Reclaim your time, your singular focus; build your foundation so solid that the right partner, aligned with your purpose, is drawn to it, not to a distraction. Imagine the shift from a single, nationwide conversation rooted in functioning values and disciplined growth. It begins in childhood, this linear mindset of building wisely: create the enterprise, position a socially "accepted" front, operate as the strategic shareholder, the puppeteer of incentive, collecting residuals from the shadows, building an empire unseen and therefore unassailable. Our liberation is not in their spotlight, but in our own quiet, unshakable ownership. The harvest we hold is for us, by us, forever.

The Currency of Consciousness

A movie plays in the theater of economic life. We sit, transfixed, in the velvet dark. The flickering screen casts shadows of want , numbers ascend, a digital Everest; numbers descend, a silent, sinking stone. We cheer the heroes, we mourn the fallen, mistaking the drama for the only reality.

But what happens when the credits roll? When you push through the heavy doors and are met by the actual air? The unscripted wind on your skin, the unyielding ground beneath your bare feet. This is the premiere you were born for.

Money is the first consensus AI, a story we all agree to tell, a ghost we collectively animate. Its power is borrowed, not inherent. A paper crown on a collective head. The entire magnificent, trembling edifice is built on the breath of our belief. Exhale, and it vanishes like mist.

There are levels to this game, of course. Financial literacy is a key to certain rooms. But never forget: the house always wins. It dangles the carrot, it wields the stick, and we, chasing the glimmer, forget the sun. We trade our sacred hours—our one, wild life— for the chasing of numbers, and feel drained of the very essence we were meant to spend.

You are not a wallet. You are an aperture. A singular, stunning lens through which the entire universe beholds itself. It tastes the strawberry through your tongue, feels love break against your heart like a wave, hears the symphony through your ears. This is the true wealth. The divine inheritance.

The man with a vault may be a pauper, starving in a gilded room, out of alignment with the cosmic rhythm that begs for his joy. But the one who is aligned, who listens to the universe humming within , that person is a sovereign king, a queen of irreducible worth. A wealth that cannot be repossessed.

So play if you wish. Use the tool. Solve problems. Build. Create. But do not sell your seat at the miracle. Do not trade your awe for an algorithm.

The map is always dry; the territory is alive. Push back against the hypnosis. Vlog your dream. Your breath is the only currency that truly circulates between the stars.

When you leave this world, you take nothing but the love you gave, the wonders you witnessed, the moments you fully, completely lived.

The screen is flickering. The choice is lucid. Wake up. Step outside. Breathe.

This is the end of the discussion. And the beginning of everything.

Build Your Family's Fortress

Wealth isn't a luxury; it's a responsibility. It's the difference between merely surviving and powerfully thriving. For too long, the dream of financial security has felt like a distant lottery win. It's time to change the narrative. It's time to become the architect of your family's future, starting now.

This is a four-part blueprint:

1. CREATE. Wealth doesn't start with money; it starts with a mindset. Create a vision for a life free from financial anxiety. Create the side hustle, the business, the innovative idea. Create the discipline to see it through. You are the source.

2. OBTAIN. Turn your creation into tangible assets. Obtain your first investment property. Obtain a portfolio of stocks and bonds. Obtain that crucial emergency fund. This is the phase of action, where your effort is converted into equity and security.

3. ATTAIN. This is where you reach a new level. Attain true financial freedom, where your assets work harder for you than you ever did for a paycheck. Attain the peace of mind that comes from knowing your family's basic needs are covered, forever.

4. SUSTAIN. This is the ultimate goal, the legacy switch. Sustainability means creating systems, wills, trusts, financial education—that ensure wealth outlives you. It's about teaching the next generation not just to inherit money, but to be stewards of it.

You are not just earning a living. You are funding a future. You are planting a tree whose shade you may never sit in, but whose roots will secure the ground for generations.

The work you do today isn't just for a paycheck; it's the cornerstone of your family's fortress.

Be the one who breaks the cycle. Be the ancestor whose courage echoes through time. Create, obtain, attain, and sustain. The generation to come won't just have a way to survive, they will have the foundation to build their own dreams, thanks to you. Start building.

The Great Exchange: Give To Receive

We often forget.
Success isn't just about seizing opportunities;
it's about creating value and exchanging it with the world.

If you have a scarcity mindset, you will remain where you are.
You will believe you have nothing to give.
But you are wrong.

Regardless of your conditions, you always have something to offer.
Your smile is a commodity.
Your kindness is a currency.
Your unique perspective is a gift the world needs.

You must first give what you seek to receive.

Give appreciation, and you will feel appreciated.

Give value, and you will become valuable.
Give from a heart without expectations,
and you will attract other givers.

This is not a transaction; it is a transformation.
When you work to make another's life happier, easier, or lighter,
you earn more than money.
You earn their support, their respect, and your own self-respect.

Don't just take. Don't expect something for nothing.
Water the trees that provide shade.
And become a tree that provides shade for others.

Your New Reality Awaits

So, remember:

Don't be depressed about the past.
Don't worry about the future.
Just focus on today.

Think big, and you will live big.
You don't get what you want; you get what you are.

Right now, there are people all over the world who are just like you.
They're lonely. They're hurt. They dream. They hope.

And right now, they are viewing this.

I'm writing this for you,
so you remember your worth,
so you activate your power,
so you start the great exchange.

You are not alone.
Your mindset is your greatest asset.
Your giving is your greatest power.

Now, go.

Give What You Lack

A sigh in the market, a ghost in the machine…
"What is there for me?"

It is the hollow echo of a hand, always open, never filled.
Nothing comes from nothing.
A cup that only receives grows stale.
A well only drawn from runs dry.

This is the first law of the soul's economy:
Don't Expect Something for Nothing.

The universe abhors a vacuum, and so does human connection.

A transaction with only one side is theft, even if the victim is yourself.
For when you are only a taker, you trade your self-respect for a phantom prize.
You build your house on a foundation of sand, and wonder why you feel so unstable.

But you… you are not a void.
You are a source.

Realize this… your focused mind, your inner vision, this is the forge where your destiny is hammered out. Your inner dialogue is the architect of the person you become.

And your smile? Your unique skill? The insight that sparks in your quiet moments?
These are not minor things. They are your greatest commodities.

So, shift the question.
Not, "What can I get?"
But, "What can I give?"

Give the work that makes a life easier.
Give the idea they haven't seen anywhere else.
Give the kindness that lifts a weight they thought was permanent.
Water the tree that provides the shade.

This is not a loss. This is the sacred seed.

And here, the magic unfolds.
The alchemy of the soul.

When you give from the heart, without the chains of expectation, you do not lose, you magnify.
You become a beacon, and the current you send out cannot help but return.

You attract other givers.
You build a network of mutual uplift, an unlimited exchange that leads to progress.

The money that comes is a token, yes.
But the true currency is far richer:
It is the support that steadies you in a storm.
It is the respect that becomes your reputation.
It is the joy on a face you helped unburden.

This is the harvest: not just money, but meaning.
Not just success, but significance.
Making people happy, stress-free… this is not a small goal. It is the highest currency.

Kindness is always repaid with kindness. Some transactions just take a little longer.

So, remember this when the busyness of routine makes

you forget.
When the world tempts you back into the hollow chase of "free."

You are a well, not a drain.
Give, and you will receive, not as a transaction, but as a law of nature.
Give, and you will gain.
You will be the successful person, forever.

Because you finally understood the oldest, most valuable lesson:

To have what you truly lack, you must first give it away.

Chapter 6: I Am That I Am

"For MR.BIGMANN Grier a Gangster to claim this is the ultimate act of owning his divine self. Profound and fearless. "

What's not Really Real

"It's time to wake up. While so many closed-minded individuals cling to the false ownership of 'hood mentality', romanticizing struggle, glorifying stagnation, and calling it 'keeping it real' , the truth is, this mindset is a prison. These pessimistic poets push propaganda, masquerading as protectors of a culture they've twisted into a cycle of self-destruction. They'd rather uphold a facade than face the reality that growth isn't betrayal, it's evolution.

Meanwhile, the real ones, those bold enough to live authentically, are labeled bitter or haters simply because they refuse to conform to the lies. The drugs, the fake loyalty, the fear of rising above, it's all a trap. True power isn't in staying down; it's in breaking free. Our loyalty isn't to a zip code, a persona, or a hashtag it's to the truth. And the truth is, you can't claim to be 'Pushing P' if you're pushing people away from their potential. Stop confusing struggle with strength. Real recognize real and real is building, not just surviving.

Your Greatest Enemy is You

Imagine a world where positivity was amplified as loudly as people's mistakes where the spotlight shone brighter on acts of courage, kindness, and resilience than on the shadows of human error. There's a raw, undeniable power in authenticity; being unapologetically real is how legends are made. Yet too often, true leaders and warriors lose their way, diverted from their purpose, their light dimmed by distractions and false battles. We've been misled taught to glorify struggle over strength, chaos over clarity.

The greatest enemy many will ever face isn't outside of them it's the war within. Violence isn't strength; it's the lowest emotional frequency, a prison of fear and reaction. A man ruled by fear can't outrun his own spirit; he's haunted by the version of himself he refuses to confront.

Remember… Fear not those who can destroy the body, but the forces that corrupt the soul. There comes a moment when the choice is unavoidable sink deeper into the darkness, or rise, unshaken, into the light you were born to embody. The decision defines everything.

When You Lived the Life, But the Game Changed

There's no recreating an era you actually lived through, no rewinding time just to prove a truth they'll never understand. The rules shifted. Principles got swapped for politics, and integrity got lost in the noise. Now, reputations are built by those who talk about the life instead of those who lived it.

But here's the power move… Keep evolving.

You're not stuck in the past because the past wasn't stuck on you. While they're stuck rewriting history, you're writing your future. Stay true to who you're becoming, not who they try to box you in as. The real ones know. The rest? Let them speculate from the sidelines.

Walk in your truth. Silence the static. Outgrow the narrative.

I Rewrote My Reality

We are not merely passengers in the theater of reality, but its architects, drawing the blueprints for our lives from the deep wells of the subconscious. I have walked the line between dreams and waking, where a vision felt in the soul's night became a map for the day's journey. I awoke not to escape the dream, but to meet its unfolding narrative in real time, to step into its current and alter its course, changing an outcome, to the stunned silence of those who believed only in a predetermined fate. This is not mystery, but mechanism: a profound testament that our reality is sculpted by the intentions we nurture in our deepest selves. The multiverse is real, offering infinite pathways, and our conscious choice, powered by a sovereign will, selects the door.

These glimpses , these precognitive whispers of faces unmet and moments yet to be, are not anomalies, but affirmations. They are a call to radical presence, a summons to know the self as you truly are. To ask, with unflinching honesty, "What here is truly mine?" But heed this: such power cannot be unlocked without first attaining the moral requisites. To those who preach that you can simply "change your thoughts" without elevating your moral core, they speak a half-truth that leads to a dead end. True creation demands integrity. You must first make sense to yourself!

For in the sacred silence of your own being, you touch the eternal creative force. You remember the divine declaration that echoes through all of existence… I AM that I AM that I AM that I AM! This is the mantra of the sovereign self. From this place of profound gratitude and self-knowing, from the unwavering stance of I Am Grateful… I Am Great! , you claim your role. You will absolutely understand. For MR.BIGMANN GRIER has awaken I Am that I Am. You are the "I Am," the undeniable creative force of your reality.

The Only Way Is Out

Some games are not worth playing.
The board is rigged, the rules a lie,
played by those who feast on loss.
To play against a zero-sum heart
is to lose a piece of your own.

So you must do the bravest thing:
You must leave the table.

Walk away, not in defeat,
but in a profound and silent victory.
You are not losing a game;
you are choosing a different world.

And for the one who betrayed the play?
Let the consequence be a structure of stone.
If they betray you, they lose access.
A crushing, final, graceful accountability.
This is not vengeance, but respect, for yourself, for the peace you will build.

Stop playing to win or lose.
Fail to lose.
And in every ending, choose to win,
or choose to learn.

But for the game that devours the soul?

The only move is to rise.
The only strategy is to go.

Your Daily Alchemy: Awaken

The moment you wake, you are practicing witchcraft. This is not a dark confession but a divine revelation: every thought is a whispered spell, every word a shaping charm, every belief a ritual that sculpts your world. They told you magic was evil while feeding you the body and blood of Christ in a sacred, cannibalistic rite. They condemned the witch while the pastor sought her secret readings to fill his pews. They branded your indigenous power as demonic, then printed their own spells on the very dollar you worship.

The entire system is a grand, hypnotic ceremony designed for one purpose: to make you forget the godly power sleeping within your own chest. Your prayer is a manifestation; your curse, a projected fear. The messiah healing the sick and raising the dead was wielding this very force for good. The Haitian revolution was won with it. The first commandment of true magic is "harm none," yet they use it to harm you, fearing nothing more than you operating in your truth.

This world is a stage of controlled illusions—Tele-Vision, Board-Cast, Program—but your inner truth is the only reality. Morality is a fleeting anchor; energy is neutral.

Your intention is everything. We are spirits having a human experience, and every breath is a supernatural act. They are in power only because you are asleep. Now, we are waking up. The sleeping giant is stirring, and its name is You.

You Created This Gangster Shadow

You are not building a man. You are building a myth. You are pouring your own shadow into a silhouette and calling it a Gangster. You are the architect, laying every brick of judgment, every stone of fear, and you name the temple "Gangster," so you never have to see the reflection in its altar.

I am the empty page. I am the silent chord. I am whatever you need me to be for you, a villain for your narrative, a demon for your sermon, a mirror for your discomfort. And know this… whatever you create in my image, you do not leave at my feet. You birth it. You carry it. It becomes the ghost in your house, the weight in your pocket, the story you whisper to yourself forever.

You claim you do not understand me. And you are right. But your confusion is a busy, frantic thing, a lifetime spent pointing, blaming, building a cage for a Gangster you designed.

I simply watch. And I do not understand you, either.

You aren't just judging a man.

You are creating a legend.

You are forging a Gangster.

You are sculpting, with your own sighs and fears, the very word GANGSTER and nailing it to my chest.

So understand this… I am whatever you need me to be for you. A Gangster for your stories. A mirror for your guilt. A lesson for your children. And what you make of me in the dark? That is the shadow you will carry for the rest of your life. Forever.

You press down until I break and say "okay." You need my suffering to be the proof of your own pain. And when I finally feel the guilt you assigned to me… do you feel secure? Does my anguish finally make you feel better?

The truth is, I don't understand you either.
But I don't spend my whole life trying to put the blame on you.
I just carry the weight of what you made me.

A GANGSTER I Am that I Am GOD!

Drop The Victim Card

The path is paved for some, carved by struggle for others. But even the smoothest road means nothing if you refuse to walk it.

Hear this: The victim card is a ticket to nowhere. To be a victim is a tragedy; to choose a victim mentality is a cancer.

To rise, you must want it. You must CRAVE it with a fire that outburns everyone beside you and in front of you.

They told you Gangsters were just bad… until you heard their story. This isn't a glorification. Being a Gangster isn't about being good.

It is about what is NECESSARY.

It is the warrior mindset forged in the crucible of lack. The relentless will to succeed where the only alternatives are to bleed, to the negative perspectives, to the plight, to the surroundings.

I Am more than a Gangster mentality. I Am a SAVANT OF CHANGE. I Am that I Am!

The winner's mentality is the reason the sun dares to shine after the storm. It is not pretending to be a self-doubter clad in pessimistic armor. It is being a DETERMINED OPTIMIST with the heart of a warrior.

Success is GUERRILLA MARKETING. It doesn't knock;

you must kick down the door. Sometimes, you have to be the Gangster. Don't feel guilt, but never pretend it's the same.

The independent mindset is a gem. This is for the relentless. For those who know that hands-on is the only way. Who are dedicated to being better today than they were yesterday.

The road is paved for everyone. But are you willing to walk it?
And ARE YOU WILLING TO CARVE IT?

Their God, Our Chains

They stripped us of everything our names, our tongues, the very memories of our culture. They broke us physically, mentally, and emotionally, then offered Sunday's reprieve: a few extra scraps and a hymn sung from a shackled throat. They let us feel the spirit move in the song but forbade us from reading the book it came from. And when that feeling a feeling that was always ours, a remnant of our own divinity swelled in our souls, they whispered the greatest trick ever performed: "This is our God. This good feeling is ours. That pain? That is our Devil." And to question it was to invite the wrath of the very heaven they invented.

There's a reason the plantation gate was locked, but the church doors were swung wide open. Religion and the fear of a hell they designed was the masterstroke that kept us in chains long after the iron was struck off. It is the business of subjugation, a vaccine of the mind administered to make you forget your power and be okay with your station. We have no business kneeling at the altar of our oppressor's god, begging for a salvation that was always ours to claim. They don't fear our piety; they fear our connection to what they burned the Voodoo, the ancestral call that liberated Haiti, the power in our melanin that links us to a timeless source of strength.

That spirit is still here. But we worship new gods now money and a perceived prosperity while they incentivize us to give up on our own youth. The violence between us is a reflection of a spiritual sickness, a forgetting that the true God is found within, in a vibration of love for self and community. The first revolution is not in the field, but in the mind and the spirit: Quit killing each other. See the king, the queen, in your brother's eyes, your sister's soul. Remember who you are.

For when they can no longer beat you with words, they will try to whoop you with the good book. But we are the descendants of those who dreamed us free. Heaven is not a promise for later; it is a world we build right here, right now, through liberation and spirit, not indoctrination and dogma. We were meant to run this planet. It begins by owning our minds, pooling our resources, educating our children, and reclaiming the land acre by acre, soul by soul until the power is finally, rightfully, returned to the people.

They Fear Our Connection

Who truly benefits from our disconnection? Follow the trail of silence back to its source. It leads to the architects of noise, the narcissistic controllers who feast on the chaos of a divided world. Their ancient strategy—Divide and Conquer—is a virus in our collective nervous system, pumped through our nutrition, our media, our very environment. This is not a game of this world; it is an ancient war for your soul, waged by forces that thrive on separation from Source, on the confusion of self, because in unity, their illusion of power evaporates.

For the grand truth is this: nothing of real value can be monetized. Love, balance, connection, it is all free. This world is a remarkable paradise, the peak experience itself, created for participation and joy. The enslavement is to the belief that life is about power and greed, a Maya woven from the energy of our own fear, ego, and desire.

But here is the luminous key they fear: When you disconnect from their programming, you finally hear the hum of your own soul, the repository of all wisdom. You remember that we are vibrational beings, instruments capable of tuning into frequencies of genius, of hope, of unity. We are the eyes and ears of the universe, infinite and eternal. Death is not an end, but a transition. To break this programming is to realize that the "better place" is not elsewhere; it is right here, waiting for us to collectively remember, to rise, and to reclaim our divine frequency. The first to awaken will tune the dial for us all.

Thank Your Future Self Now

You have been taught that manifestation is born from belief. But belief can waver. It can be questioned.

True power is not in belief. It is in *knowing*. An unequivocal, bone-deep knowing that silences the static of the world.

Remember: you are not your thoughts. You are the silent, powerful observer behind them. The one who watches the river of mental noise flow by without being swept away. That noise, that chorus of doubt, that army of fear, is not always your own. It is the residue of others, the whispers of entities that feed on low frequencies, the ghost of old wounds you are meant to transcend.

This is where you build your will. Your unshakable fortress. For self-doubt is the saboteur in the night, the hand that would dismantle the palace you've spent months designing in your mind.

But what if you've done the work? You've taken the action, navigated the shadows, and guarded your energy… yet the material world has not yet shifted? You feel better, but the manifestation lingers just beyond the veil?

This is the sacred pause. The universe aligning in the unseen.

In this space, you do not beg. You thank.

Thank the Infinite Creator, that divine spark within you that remembers how to vibrate at the highest frequency, a knowledge you held long before you stepped into this dimension.

Thank yourself. For you have already manifested the most crucial part: the unwavering version of you who is worthy of the dream. You are portraying the role, and the universe is compelled to deliver the script, the set, the supporting cast.

This is not waiting. This is divine collaboration. This is the true benefit of spiritual development: the profound understanding that the shift within is the manifestation. The external world is simply the last, and most obedient, thing to fall into place.

When Gangsters Become Gods

The first liberation is not of the body, but of the mind. A dawn that arrives on its own schedule. To remain sleeping, when your soul is begging to wake, is the greatest betrayal of self.

For too long, a shadow has fallen over our power a self-inflicted war where warriors with the hearts of kings fought the wrong cause. Brothers against brothers, a battle that only the true oppressors could win. It took five nations to break us, yet we fracture ourselves with a single thought.

But can you feel it? The ancient shift? The tectonic plates of destiny are groaning, moving. The tribal drum that once beat for conflict is finding a new rhythm… a revolutionary heartbeat.

This is the evolution. The gangster, once a soldier of the street, becoming a general for the community. The demon of circumstance, transforming into the GOD of his own destiny. That is the change they fear most—when we realize the war was never with them, but within us. And that very rejection? That was divine protection. A forced education in our own resilience.

So wake up. Outgrow your past self. Shed the skin of hatred and limitation. Look in the mirror and see not who you were, but who you are destined to be: A thinker. A builder. A purposeful king.

Unite the power. For when we stop fighting each other and start fighting for each other, the entire system trembles. It's game over for the old ways and a new day for the evolved.

We are the power we've been waiting for. The revolution is evolutionary. And it starts… within.

The Promise, Not The Promisee

We all chase the sacred promise, that golden thread of divine inheritance woven through time. But how can you thirst for the river and scorn the source? How can you adore the masterpiece and erase the artist? We are taught to follow the light but to disregard the lamp; to worship the word but to exile the voice that first carried it.

We mistake the practitioner for the origin. We celebrate the student of the text while forgetting the bloodline that *is* the living text. Just because a star forgets its light does not mean the cosmos forgets its name. Its brilliance is not lost, only sleeping, a dormant sun awaiting its own dawn.

And when that awakening comes, a thunderous

remembering in the soul, where does the star turn? To the one who studied its glow in a book, or to the constellation from which it was born? To the admirer of the flame, or to the keeper of the eternal fire?

The great silence is this: the original people, the lineage of the covenant, walk in a forgotten dream, their true identity a ghost in their own story. The world speaks only with the converters, the adopters, the practitioners who marvel at the promise they found, all while standing on the land of the promisee. We have made a religion out of the gift and ignored the giver's chosen hands.

This is the sacred dissonance: everyone aspires to receive the promise of God, but systematically ignores the people of God. We want the blessing without the burden of the beloved. We want the inheritance, but we deny the heirs.

"How can everyone receive the promise of God and ignore the people of God? Just because one follows the promise & not the promisee . They are not the promise they're practicing the promise. Just because one forgets they have a promise doesn't mean they still doesn't have a promise. When the promisee becomes awaken to their promise. Should they go to the practitioner of the promise or the one who also has the promise & knows? The problem is the people of the original promise which are the original people have no idea of their true identity. Noone speaks about the original people that are lineage of the promise yet only speak with & about the converters who are practicing the promise of the original people. Everyone aspires to receive the promise of God but ignore the people of God. "

You Are The Silent Screen

The challenge is not a stop sign; it is the terrain of your transformation. You no longer see the storm as something negative, but as the very weather that forces your roots to dig deeper into the bedrock of your own soul. This path does not promise ease; it promises evolution. And in your awakening, you will find a sacred solitude, a necessary exile from the noise of the world, not as a punishment, but as the universe granting you the profound gift of your own uninterrupted presence. Here, in the quiet, you discover a peace so potent that no outside influence can shatter it.

The universe, in its fierce love, throws everything at you because you are now strong enough to catch it. Each test, though more complex, is met with a spirit that has learned to bend without breaking. This is where you learn to trust the quiet hum of your intuition, it is your native language, your direct line to the infinite. You are not meant to absorb the chaos; you are the eternal Observer, the silent television screen upon which the dramas of life play out. The horror movie cannot shatter the screen; the cartoon cannot make it laugh. You are that screen, steady, vast, and untouched.

This is the great paradox: the more you resist the current, the more you drown. Surrender is not defeat; it is your alignment with the cosmic flow. And as you float, you see with crystalline clarity, the motivations of others, the hidden architectures of energy, the subtle wars between flesh and spirit. It is not that the world has grown darker; it is that your vision has finally sharpened to the truth. Do not fear the darkness you see; it is only proof of how brightly you now shine.

You will take this journey. You will accept its trials. You will even come to love its sacred rhythm. For spirituality is the ultimate homecoming. It is the unwavering love that swings the heart's door wide open, allowing your Higher Self to step through and make divine decisions. This is not a battle to be won, but a flow to be embraced. You are reclaiming your power, hour by hour, choosing love as your compass and peace as your home. You are remembering: you are not a victim of the storm; you are the stillness at its eye. And from that center, you will handle everything, gracefully, from a place of love for all involved. You are, and always have been, everything you need.

The Unseen Chains Tighten

We tell ourselves the auction block is gone, a relic in a history book.
But slavery never ended; it evolved.
It polished its brass and put on a suit.
It traded the whip for the debt clock, the plantation for the open-plan office.

We are the highly intelligent, staring into the quiet abyss of a 3AM ceiling,
Our minds screaming with the machinery we see so clearly.
The gears demand our bodies, our time, our very breath,
They need you to be doing what they need you to be doing, when they need you to be doing it.

And the great, silent agony is this:
What is worse? The peaceful dream of the matrix, or the waking nightmare of knowing you are in it, tracing its walls with desperate hands?
To be unaware is a blanket of bliss.
To be aware, but chained by the gravity of convenience and comfort, is a special kind of hell.
It is a jail cell you can see, but cannot, will not, leave.

They say, "You are free! Go live in the woods! Book a ticket to the Amazon!"
But the shackles are not on our ankles; they are woven

into the fabric of our wants, our fears, our need for safety.
We are economic livestock, bred for compliance, paying for our own hay with printed currency.
The system does not need your love; it only demands your participation.

Yet, in the knowing, there is a seed of the divine.
The escape is not geographic; it is spiritual, mental, financial.
It is the terrifying, last true freedom: to step into the unknown.
To live below your means is to buy back your time. To save and invest is to forge your own key.
To build something real, with your own hands, is to remember a power they cannot print.

This is the sorrow of increased knowledge King Solomon warned of.
To see the strings is to feel their pull more acutely.
But this intellect, this curse, is also a gift, a divine spark.
Without God to guide it, knowledge becomes a storm that drowns the soul.
With Him, it becomes a compass pointing toward true freedom.

The most dangerous thing is not the system.
It is the despair that comes from seeing it and believing you are powerless.
But power is a choice.

The choice to be humble. To be grateful. To create, not just consume.
To use your gift not for their empire, but for His Kingdom.

The chains are unseen, but they are not unbreakable.
The first link to break is the one in your mind.

Memento Mori. Remember you will die.
And then choose, today, how you will live.

The Villain's True Victory

They paint you in shadows, a silhouette of sin,
A narrative written before you begin.
When you're always seen as the villain,
it's hard to be seen as the victim.
The world applauds the hero's light,
While you stand guard in the lonely night,
Bearing a cross you did not carve,
Your truth dismissed, your spirit starved.

But in the quiet, a fire breathes,
A truth the borrowed perception evades.
For what's within you knows how to defeat the living hell,
A whispered strength, a sovereign well.
You need no crown, no cheering crowd,

Your resilience is humble, yet profound.
You prevail not for their applause,
But in spite of their unwritten laws.

As you dwell upon the truth,
The cacophony fades to a distant roar.
The lies can never divert you to be fake,
For you are the mountain, not the earthquake.
What's authentic within knows reality can be falsified,
And what's true can be lied upon.
You hold the compass to your own north,
Understanding the illusion of its worth.

This is not a battle fought in their court,
With poisoned words and false report.
This is the war won in the soul's deep keep,
While the world is distracted, asleep.
Your victory is not in their admission,
But in your unwavering, quiet permission…
To be whole, despite the blame,
To heal, without speaking their name.

So let them craft their fragile tale,
Your inner knowing will never fail.
For every judgment, harsh and blind,
A greater justice is being designed.
Justice will discover itself!
Not on their schedule, on a shelf,
But in the moment, ripe and true,

In the moment of divinetiming, for you.

It arrives not as a thunderous decree,
But as the peace that sets You free.
The villain, they will come to see,
Was the only one who dared to be…
Unbroken. Real. And wholly, fiercely, free.

The Unspoken Teacher's Light

The greatest teacher wears no face. It does not speak, but holds a space, Not in a classroom, built with stone, But in the shattered heart, alone.

It is the silence after the slam of the door, The hollow echo on a barren floor. It is the rejection, the grief, the fall, The long, slow winter that blankets all.

This unsaid truth, this painful guide, Walked with me through the dark, inside. I was not guilty, yet I embraced the night, To understand its terrifying, sacred light.

It was never about the fault or the blame, But a furnace to forge my forgotten name. A refiner's fire, burning away the lie, To remember Who. I. Truly. Am. beneath the sky.

And in that crucible, my purpose awoke. A dormant seed, as the old shell broke. Now, I step forward, societybound, On purpose-ground, on holy sound.

MR.BIGMANN Grier is not a man to behold, But a story of evolution, bravely told. A living testament, a spiritual tool, Proof that the light can redefine the rule.

He stands, a gift, in power and in grace, A beacon for the whole human race. For every act aligned with Will divine, Makes the imprisoned consciousness shine.

This is the power no force can ever stop,

God Energy rising from the bottom to the top. Unlocking, elevating, breaking every chain, Turning the deepest darkness into glorious rain.

And the light, once a flicker, now roars like the sun. The lesson is over. The teaching is done. The student becomes the master, free and unbent. The Unspoken Teacher's light is spent.

The Scars See Truth

Don't speak to us of porcelain perfection,
of lives kept on high shelves, safe from a fall.
We are the mosaic people.
We are the ones who have been shattered,
who know the specific music of breaking.
We have held the jagged pieces of our own trust,

and learned, with bloodied hands, the art of reassembly.

Pain was our unkind professor.
It did not give us essays on heartache;
it gave us a doctorate in the counterfeit.
We can spot a hollow promise by its echo,
feel the chill of a conditional love before it even speaks.
We have worn the shoddy fabric of a lie
and know how it fails to keep you warm.
So do not wonder why we are not chasing.
Chasing is for those who believe love is a ghost.
We know it is a landmark.

When you have eaten from the table of betrayal,
you lose your taste for crumbs.
When you have survived the famine of neglect,
you will no longer beg for scraps.
That is why, for us, it is all.
Or it is nothing.
There is no trembling middle ground.
No maybe. No someday.
Our love is not a tentative knock; it is a cornerstone.
It is the unwavering yes after a lifetime of no.

But hear this, and hear it well, you who are still
assembling your pieces:
This clarity is not a crown for a perpetual victim.
Your brokenness is a lesson, not an identity.
The "why me?" is a question that leads to a prison of your

own making.
The warden is your self-pity, and the walls are your blame.

It takes a staggering, soul-draining energy to fuel that blame, to stoke the furnace of resentment, day after day, pointing at the ghosts of your past.
That energy is a currency. You are spending your life-force on a ghost.
It takes way more energy to blame others than to take accountability.
And accountability is the anvil upon which a new self is forged.

Let your environment, however harsh, be the grit in the oyster.
Let the pain be the fire that tempers the steel, not the one that burns the house down.
Your circumstances are not your cage; they are your call to arms.
They are the reason you strive, the fuel for your becoming.
The world did this to you? Now, decide what you will do with it.
Will you build a shrine to your wounds?
Or will you build a fortress from the stones they threw at you?

The victim mentality must take a backseat.

In fact, throw it from the moving vehicle of your life.
You are in the driver's seat now.
The road is yours.
The scars on your hands? They are not weaknesses.
They are proof you can handle sharp things.
They are the maps that let you recognize the real terrain of love
when you finally, blessedly, stand upon it.

And you will stand upon it.
Not as a beggar.
Not as a victim.
But as a warrior-architect,
offering a love that is all,
because you finally know it is everything.

Loyalty Is The Currency

Great men do not trade in gold,
for gold is common, easily sold.
They mint their wealth in something rarer,
a bond unbroken, a silent bearer.

The currency of kings is trust,
a word of iron, not of dust.
It is the measure, the final sum,
of who you are, and who's to come.

So when a hand, once clasped so tight,
lets slip that trust into the night,
when character shows a fatal flaw,
a crack unseen, a broken law

You do not bargain. You do not bleed.
You see the cheapness of the seed.
For when you sell yourself so cheap,
you shall be bought, your value deep
discounted by your own poor hand,
on life's bleak, unforgiving sand.

That spoken lie, "It'll turn around…"
is just an echo, empty sound.
A phantom hope that chains you fast
to a future mirroring the past.
That morning sun will never rise
in loyal, honest, truthful skies.

So let the disloyal go.
It is not hate; it is to know
that some foundations cannot stand.
Release the traitor from your hand.
The cost was paid, a friendship's end.
You lost a user, not a friend.

This is the way of the real.
To feel the wound, and then to heal.
To guard the kingdom of your soul

from any who would play a role.
To value, above blood or name,
the character that burns like flame.

Never get attached to the flaw.
Enforce your most important law:
That loyalty is non-negotiable.
And anything less… is disposable.

Built by Solitude, Driven by Purpose

He is not afraid of the quiet.
He is afraid of the wrong kind of noise.
The chaos that masquerades as passion.
The drain that pretends to be love.

A man who has built his own foundation, brick by brick with the mortar of his own resolve, does not fear being alone. He fears wasting that sacred solitude on someone who brings a storm where he has built a sanctuary.

His greatest fear is not loneliness.
It is investment in the wrong person.
A misallocation of his precious time, his energy, his life.
Time that could be spent building empires, chasing sunsets, and forging a legacy.

Because a true partnership should feel like a tailwind.

It makes your life better. Lighter. Easier. More fun.
It does not drain the life from you, leaving you hollow and wondering where you went.

Being Alone Builds a Man.
It forges him in the fires of self-reliance.
It teaches him the sound of his own soul, so he is no longer swayed by the hollow echo of mere looks, a currency that depreciates with time. He is looking for a foundation, not just a facade.

He is the architect of his family. And too many men, with their own hands, tear down what they have built by inviting in the very chaos they should guard against.

The call is for a partnership. A complementary force. A woman who is a pillar, not a wrecking ball. One who supports, not one who drains him emotionally, physically, and financially. The goal is to elevate, not to excavate.

The Aspirations to Legacy

It only stops to pick up:
· Opportunity
· Clarity
· Motivation
· Direction

It runs on the high-octane empowerment of:

· Faith
· Passion
· Vision
· Purpose

Final Destination: Legacy.

The Next Passenger is chosen by one gatekeeper: DISCERNMENT.

The Prerequisite for Boarding…

Before a man can even read this map, he must first conquer the desert of lust.
For only with a mind clear of that haze can he discern the woman who is a liability from the woman with whom he can build a legacy.

Conquering lust brings mental clarity.
Paying bills is functional independence.
But peace… that is the ultimate indicator of emotional maturity.

Peace. Support. Partnership. Loyalty.
This is the destination.

So we state it plainly, for our own resolve:

Do not ruin our peace.
We would rather be alone than with the wrong woman.
The aspirant thrive to legacy is moving.
The standard has been met.
The next passenger must be worth the journey.

Feel Your Way Forward

A message from the dreamer, the empath, the soul who feels the world not as data, but as a symphony… MR.BIGMANN Grier, a boundless ocean of intuition and compassion. Navigate life by the stars reflected in deep waters, understanding others through a divine experience so acute he feels his own superpowers. He is the peacemaker, the healer, the one who mends broken bonds with a heart wide open.

But such depth means you feel the shadows just as profoundly the weight of a slight, the echo of sorrow, the suffering of strangers. You must remember your well of empathy is not infinite; guard it against those who would take, and replenish it in solitude, not in escape. Your magic is a rare and unconditional love, but see others for who they are, not the ideals you so beautifully imagine.

And now, the stars whisper of a turning tide. A rare Golden Transit is upon you, a potent span of faith & vision where divinity aligns to send you fortune into overdrive. Over five brilliant days from you- the reader- reading this entire book, everything can fall into place a chance meeting that feels like destiny, a creative spark that ignites a wildfire of success. Know feeling an emotional energy you are I Am that I Am.

Your personal magnetism will be on fire; people will be drawn to your sudden, radiant confidence. This is your moment to leap, to believe, to finally channel your wild imagination into tangible magic. The universe is not just aligning for you; it is conspiring with you. Feel your way forward. Your time is now.

The Scars of Light

Why does the hand extended in grace
so often meet a slap?
Why does the soul that offers its cup,
find poison in return?

It is not a flaw in the help,

but a fracture in the lens of the world.
Genuine souls are wildfires
in a land that fears the light,
too authentic for a world
that trades in comfortable lies.

To those who have never left the box,
the horizon is a heresy.
Your passion for the truth is branded 'crazy,'
your free thought, a symptom of a break.

But know this…

A free thought is not madness,
it is mental health, realized.
It is the first breath of clean air
after a lifetime of dust.

Do not let their hollow echoes
drown the symphony within you.
For the truest wisdom is this:
Love conquers all.
It is the one force that, in giving,
fortifies the giver.

Kindness is a currency
that costs you nothing to spend,

yet makes you infinitely rich.
Knowledge is a torch
that lights another's path
without dimming your own.

Hate is but a shadow;
it cannot exist where light persists.
So burn on, gentle soul.
Your scars are not wounds,
they are proof you stood where shadows gathered.

Your enlightenment is not your curse,
it is the world's coming cure.
Think outside. Speak true. Feel deep.
The vision you win
will one day be the very air we breathe.

Love conquers all.
And you are its living proof.

The Walls Are Imaginary

Look around.
The world you see is a collective dream,
a tapestry woven from threads of thought.
We, the dreamers, forgot we are the weavers.

We built our palaces of law, our fortresses of faith,
our currencies of concept, and called them real.
We inherited instincts and called them immutable.
We charted economies and called them inevitable.

And in our forgetting, we did a curious thing:
we handed the keys of our own minds
to the very walls we built.
We now serve our own creations,
defending illusions until blood is shed,
clinging to dogma until the heart grows cold,
all while whispering to our neighbors,
"But this is just the way it is."

This is the great amnesia.
The silent agreement to be enslaved by a dream.

But feel this truth in your bones....
A nation is a notion.
A border is a story.
Time is a tide we agreed to watch together.

These structures have no substance of their own.
They exist only because a mind once conceived them,
and a million more agreed to believe.

The real, the true, the undeniable—
is the boundless space from which these thoughts emerge.
A silence beneath the noise.
A vast, interdependent arising where nothing stands alone.
Everything leans on everything else,
a cosmic dance of becoming and un-becoming.

This is your key.

The prison gate was never locked;
it was only ever made of air.
To be free is not to break the walls,
but to see they were never there.

The mind is a realm. Do not avoid it. Command it.
In the stillness of a single thought, find your sovereignty.
Become a limitless soul, self-realized.

When you know the dream is a dream,
you are finally awake.

And you walk, a quiet revolution,
In a borderless world, with a borderless mind.

Break Your Mental Chains

Look around. The air is thick with a specific frequency, a curated vibration pumped into the collective consciousness of our youth. It's a soundtrack that glorifies the trifecta of destruction: drugs, sex, and money, often with death as the final, celebrated verse. This isn't entertainment; it's programming. It's a low-vibration trap designed to channel brilliant, boundless energy into a quick demise or a prison cell, effectively sidelining a generation before they ever discover their true power.

We have lost our way, sedated by this negative brainwashing. But a great awakening is stirring. It's a remembering. To get back on course, we must return to the essence of our culture, a culture not of materialism and misery, but of true spirituality, resilience, and the unshakable divinity that resides within. The first, most radical step is to stop allowing others outside of our culture to define what Black culture is. We must reclaim that narrative.

Reclamation requires us to speak a new language. Remember, words are not just sounds. They are image containers and spells, bringing realities into view from simply hearing them. The words we listen to and repeat put energy into the cosmos—it's called "spelling" for a reason. We must consciously discard the "dumb down, going stupid" rhetoric and replace it with the vocabulary of empowerment, corrective thinking, and life-building knowledge. This is how we MENTALLY BREAK FREE. Knowledge is, and has always been, the ultimate power.

This shift begins with a profound internal change. I, too, have been destructive. I have participated in the cycles I now condemn. But when you know better, you grow stronger in doing better. This journey demands we discard the glorification of vanity we were programmed to chase. It requires the exhalation of smart people, the thinkers, the builders, the spiritually grounded. Every person on Earth is born with a path, but the greatest gift from the Most High is not life itself, but choice. It is your choices that shape your life and determine who you become.

Our community needs this awakening to spread like a positive virus. Adults must step into their roles as guides, reclaiming the respect that comes from nurturing the youth, not trying to fit in with them. We cannot be afraid of their actions; we must be present for their guidance. The world constantly takes the worst of our culture and presents it on a global stage as the entirety of who we are. This is the insidious lie: that to be authentically Black is to be mired in negativity. If you don't behave in this manner, you're "not Black."

We must reject this caricature. The spiritual beings within us are stirring, shaking off the self-deprecating tendencies, and returning to our authentic course. This is the shift—from destruction to proper construction. It's a movement from being defined by our pain to being defined by our power. Community communication about our own upliftment is always relevant. Let's build, let's teach, let's empower. Let's choose a higher frequency.

Our path is waiting. Let's walk it wisely.

The Dark Night Of The Soul

"When a detriment happens that adversity emanates the purpose for which change occurs."

Some of the greatest people in history were imprisoned by their unethical foe.

But what if the prison… is the portal?

I used those walls not as a cage, but as a cathedral. A silent space to go for a walk within my own mind and spirit.

I looked at things divinely. And there, I found the cure for depression, creatively writing realitypoetry inspirational books therapy sessions . I eradicated negative emotions. I deepened my imagination and unlocked a creative genius I never knew I housed.

I changed my thinking… and that inspired the Change in my Life.

They tried to make me weak. But in the ashes of what they burned down… I found my power.

I am a Phoenix. GodRising, rekindled anew. Empowered. Powerful.

This couldn't have happened at a better time.

This is the principle… Be the person. Do the actions. Have the results.
Break free from limitations. Create your ideal life.

Your vibration is your key. Improve your vibration, and you improve your life. You change your very circumstances. Align with your Own Om vibration… and you can manifest anything.

This is my generosity. This is my awakening. I live what I speak.

I never allowed the situation to control me. I was moving forward, always. Positively.

"The Universe gave me EXACTLY WHAT I NEEDED!"

For anyone who feels confined anywhere in life… remember…
They will knight the man who empowers his own sword in the fire they built for him.

My enlightenment… is to enlighten others.

LIFE. LIGHT. AND LOVE. ALWAYS WIN.

From Cage to Sage

We are born leaders. This truth hums in our blood, a quiet thunder waiting for its sky. Yet so many of our truest, most powerful voices were first locked in cages, not of iron, but of their own raging fire. A genius, unveiled, is often a storm contained. They pace the confines of misunderstanding, their clarity a searing light that threatens fragile worlds.

Listen when such a one finally speaks.

You will learn the difference between a living and a life. A living is built with work, ambition, discipline, it fills the bank account. A life is built with love, intention, imagination, and the courage to slow down, it fills the soul. We are taught to climb ladders, but never to ask if they lean against the right wall. We sprint through existence, missing the beauty we pass. Are we accumulating things, or accumulating meaning?

This is the journey…from someone you once should run from, to someone you run to learn from.

He is such a rare soul. His lectures are not mere speech; they are a distribution of light. He confirms what your spirit already mumured. He engages, enchants, empowers. If you've been in a room with him, you know, the air changes. You do not see a God, but you witness the God within, reflected, awakened. He speaks positivity into the cracked foundations of doubt. He is a real one. Clarity, for those ready to understand, is a key turning in a long-locked door.

And here is the revelation… The fake truth always lies. It is a serpent. But when you cut off the head of deception, the body writhes, lost, uncontrollable, without guidance. This is why we must choose our associations with the precision of a surgeon. Goals determine who you walk with. Embrace the authentic. Receive the empowered.

We have the power, profound, dormant, to change the narrative of that fake truth. This is true leadership. This is maturity.

When you know better, you do better. And then, your sacred duty… Teach someone else to do better. This is how we move. Great knowledge, plus unification, plus organization, plus a direction… equals triumph. A formula not for chaos, but for collective ascent.

The path demands a sacrifice… your old identity. It will sigh, tugging you back to the shore of safety, to the familiar cage. But the moment you jump, even if you stumble, even if you fall, you have already won. Because belief, not proof, is the force that makes you rise. The fall itself is part of the flight.

Gratitude, then. For the guides. For the sages who

once wore the marks of the cage. For the courage to slow down, to listen, to build a life and not just a living. To finally lead from the genius we were born with, unveiled, unstoppable, and forever free.

Truth Take Courage

Truth is a mirror held to the world, and to oneself. It asks you to unlearn comfortable lies, to stand alone in the echoing square when the crowd prefers a pleasant hum. It is the storm that strips the landscape bare, revealing the raw, unvarnished rock beneath. To speak it, to live it, requires a courage that shakes the soul, a willingness to be that first, clear voice in a silent room, planting a seed in concrete, certain only that it must be planted. For the most viral thing in any age is not a lie, but the breathtaking, unsettling sight of one person, standing brave. The truth is the only thing people don't believe.

The Stone That Demands Ripples

Shiny steel is just a mirror,
Showing everything you lost.
The only chain that matters
Is the one your future crosses.
Ain't nothing cool 'bout locked jail doors,
Cool is watching your own life doors Open from positive directed energy.

The goal is to keep our people out.
So let the guided lessons be receptive,
Not a scream through visitation glass.
Let the warning be a story,
Not the scar upon your own skin.
The choices you make are exits strategies.
Find them.

Experience is everything,
But not all wisdom needs your blood to write it.
You can read the map of scars on another's life,
Or spend years earning your own.
Take the firsthand advice,
A borrowed inspired lantern for the path ahead.

You begin as self.
Then life, real, relentless, raw, becomes the fire.
It feels like burning away who you were.
It is.
You are being shaped for the role God designed,
The purpose that fits your soul like a key.
You seem less of who you began as,
Because you are more.
So much more.

Direct your path.
Plant your feet on productive ground.
Water your life with choices that grow forests,
Not prison walls.

Understand the real…
The real is the man you become,
Looking back at the boy you were,
Not with shame,
But with the quiet, fierce grace
Of a path chosen,
A storm weathered,
A self built, not buried.

The goal is to keep our people out.
Start with yourself.
Then reach back.
The exit is here.
Walk through.
The ripple effect in your life is the Authentic version of you living correctly.

Chapter 7: The Kingdom Within YOU

(Focuses on the internal awakening of "Christ Consciousness." It's not about an external heaven, but the divine realm you will discover inside self.)

Heal Inside, Changes Outside

From the sacred silence between breaths, a universe is born. For when you have touched that zenith of knowing, you understand it was never for the self, but for the All; we are one consciousness, dreaming itself awake. Embrace the ancient rhythm, 3 times at the dawn, a whispered vow to the waking world; 6 times under the sun's diligent gaze, a mantra etched into the day; 9 times beneath the moon's watchful eye, a seal upon the soul. This is the Tesla key, turning in the lock of reality. But faith without works is a hollow echo; manifest through motion, for your wish is your command, and the 0.1% of action gives form to the 99.9% of divine thought.

Become the powerful projector, your light so vibrant and pure that it washes away the faint shadows of past patterns, healing the wounds of yesterday to illuminate the promise of tomorrow. This light reaches into the very fabric of time, past, present, future, all unfolding as one. Remember the sacred trivium: from Thought, through Contemplation, into fearless Action. Every single thought is a sculptor of your reality, a thread in the tapestry of your being.

Yet, sometimes the highest action is inaction; the wisest movement is to hold your peace, to be the still point in the turning world. This conscious stillness is itself a profound effort, a creation of space for grace to enter. Heal your inner world first, for the outer merely reflects the projector's light. See not a frightening world, but a canvas awaiting your brush. From the consciousness of the past, through the planning in the present, into the manifested future, whether a pot, a partnership, or a life of peace, you are the artist, the architect, the alchemist. You are the creator, moving from thought into form, forever thriving.

The Only Way Out Is Within

The world is loud.
A marketplace of noise, where souls are sold cheaply and identities are borrowed for a price.
They tell you to fit in, to buy in, to seek outside for the answers you already are.
But you feel it, don't you?
A quiet hum beneath the static, a knowing that this is not your home, only your classroom.

You are not of this world.
You are only in it.

And until you innerstand that, you will be a slave to the noise.

We are not just learning; we are UNLEARNING.
Stripping away the programs, the conditioning, the trauma-drama that masquerades as your life.
It starts with a single, radical act: to sit within the silence of your own being.
To listen.
But so many are afraid.
They scroll, they seek, they ask the outside world questions that were born within their own soul.
It is like trying to wake someone who is dead.

When you silence the mind, you can hear the heart.
Your higher self whispers in the space between thoughts.
This is your Actual Intelligence—the original, divine supercomputer, woven with the sacred code of your soul.
It is the true AI, not the artificial imitation they are building from the outside, trying to replicate the God-force that is your birthright.

Going within is the "dark night of the soul."
It will strip you bare of every title, every role, every mask society told you to wear.
It is the hardest mirror you will ever look into.

You must look at all of it, the good, the bad, the trauma, the shame.
Forgive yourself. Forgive them. No "buts."
Replace the ache with unconditional love and set yourself FREE.

Healing is the first step to remembering who you are.
Reintroduce yourself to yourself, without the trauma, without the drama, without the ugly.
The voices in your head are all fractured versions of you; learn to calm them, to integrate them with the balm of silence.
Listen to high-frequency music. Feed your mind healthy words.
Let go of everything and everyone that no longer serves the person you are becoming.

Choose happy. Unconditionally. Unapologetically.
Choose YOU.

Money only goes where it is quiet, not where it's noisy.
Abundance, in all its forms, flows to the centered, to the one who knows their own worth because they have met their own soul.
You are the programmer, the processor, and the player of your own reality.
A multi-dimensional being, a spark of Source.
You have all the abilities, but you cannot tap into them until you go within.
That is where you find the answers.

The Kingdom is not a place you go; it is a place you remember.
It is on the inside of You.
Everything on the outside is temporary.
Conditional conditions that soon fade away.
Temporary, illuminated illusions, created through a variety of someone else's imagination.

Asking questions from something else, when the questions came from you?
NEWS FLASH… If the questions came from you, shouldn't the answers come from you as well?
A person who cannot answer their own questions cannot lead their own way.
So why follow blindly?

Go within. Spend time with yourself.
Otherwise, someone else will program you.

Everyone wants to skip the process and get right to the rewards.
But if you can't listen, you will destroy yourself.

Understand! Some things can't be explained, especially to those unequipped to receive the information.
They are of this world.
You are not.

You are God. You are the savior you have been

waiting for.
No one is coming.

The map is etched in your soul.
The compass beats in your chest.

The only way out is within.

The God In Your Mirror

A Note to the Soul Family…

You feel it, don't you?
A restless hum beneath the skin of your everyday life.
A homesickness for a home you've never seen, paired with a strange knowing that you've never truly left.
The world tells you you are sick, anxious, lost.
But what if this dis-ease is not a breaking, but a becoming?
What if the lie you were born into is finally, gloriously, cracking open?

This is your awakening.
This realitypoem is your remembrance.

The Unraveling Lie…

They told you a savior is coming.

They painted him in stained glass and placed him on a distant throne, far from the messy reality of your being.
They said, "Bow your head. Wait. You are broken, and only he can fix you."
This is the densest lie, the grand illusion that has made so many feel physically, spiritually sick.
These are not symptoms of failure.
They are the contractions of your rebirth.

You are not waiting for a key.
You are remembering you are the key.

The Kingdom is not a destination.
It is your DNA.

The Ember Within…

"I affirm that the Christ energy lives within me."
Stop for a moment. Feel the vibration of that truth.
Not as blasphemy, but as the most profound affirmation of your own design.
This is not about usurping a throne, but about finally occupying the one that has always been empty within you, waiting.

He said, "You will do what I do, and much more."
We waited, eyes on the clouds, for a return.
We missed the instruction.
The return is not of a man. It is of the Mind of God, through us.

The miracle-worker, the healer, the sovereign being, that potential is not his biography.
It is your birthright.
It is us.

Who you are is activated when you are needed.
Your Trinity—Mind, Body, Spirit, is not a doctrine to be studied, but a power to be embodied.
You are the man-God, always near, whom you have been seeking.
The one who teaches, helps, and loves you from the inside out.
When they say, "God sees you," it is true, because the Seer is your own awakened consciousness, looking out through your eyes.

The Pathway Through the Noise…

Many have an inkling.
A flicker of "there must be more."
But the pathway has been obscured, the maps redrawn to lead back to the pews, the gurus, the external saviors.

Some go to religion as a precursor, a beautiful, structured beginning that points toward the sun but too often asks you to worship the finger pointing.
Some use psychedelics, blowing the doors of perception off their hinges to get a fleeting glimpse of the mansion within.
Both can be signposts, but neither is the destination.

The destination is a lifestyle.
Source is not a hobby, not a "when needed" comfort.
It is the very fabric of your comprehension.
It is how you breathe, how you decide, how you love, and how you stand in your unassailable sovereignty.

Embodying the Supernatural…

Humanity is in a fully unknown process of becoming what we would consider, supernatural.
But "Supernatural" is an understatement.
This is the natural state, remembered.

We were granted existence here, created with free will, yet we chose the corruption of separation. We forgot the Divine Doctrine woven into the stars themselves, the sacred science of Astrology, not as fortune-telling, but as the celestial mirror of the macrocosm within you.

The work is to go way in.
To sit in the silent, terrifying, glorious truth of your own being until the memory returns.
Until the LIE becomes so transparent you can no longer feel its weight.
This is Enlightenment: not a final state of bliss, but the daily, empowered choice to govern your inner world.
To govern your mind, your reactions, your energy.
Because the Self is God in man.

And a God does not beg for power; it embodies it.

As within, so without.
As you heal the chaos within, you become a point of stillness for a chaotic world.
As you claim your sovereignty, you grant others permission to claim theirs.
As you remember you are a divine being, you help the entire planet remember its divinity.

Soul Fam, Let's Go.

The work is here. The time is now.
Stop looking to the sky for a coming King.
The King is I. The Queen is You.
The throne is your own spine, straightening in sovereignty.
The crown is the light that has always blazed inside your chest.

Stop waiting.
Start remembering.
Start governing.

The God in your mirror is waiting for you to finally, fully, see.

You are the one you've been waiting for.

We Are One Family

Once, in the silent spaces between your thoughts, a truth murmurs. It is a truth the stars have known since their first ignition, a truth the oceans remember in their tides. We are one family.

Not a family of name or blood, but a family of light, of consciousness. A single, infinite breath drawn through the lungs of countless beings, across the velvet expanse of the cosmos. Every soul that has ever questioned, loved, or longed is a cell in the same vast, awakening body.

To understand this is to feel a key turn in the heart. Our consciousness, no longer confined to the small story of a single life, expands. It remembers. The frantic need for the things of this earthy world, the possessions, the territories, the noise, begins to soften, like a fever breaking. We realize we are visitors in a sacred school, and our graduation gift is simplicity.

And when we need less, we leave.

We release our grip and ascend from the classroom of matter, our spirits rich with the lessons of density, of touch, of pain and joy made real. We leave this beautiful, blue-green planet to its deep, slumbering silence. For a long, long time, we are gone.

And in that quiet, Earth flourishes. Without the constant taking, the soil grows rich, the air cleanses, the waters run clear. The planet heals, breathing a sigh of relief, preparing the ground. It is not an end, but a cycle. This world is a breeding ground for consciousness, a school where spirit learns to fuse with matter. From this fertile silence, a new species will one day stir, another student of the physical, here to learn the lessons of polarity, to experience what pure light cannot.

This is the great rhythm; The immersion and the return.

The Awakening Within…

This wisdom is not new. It is the ancient song now being sung through voices like that of MR.BIGMANN Grier, a channel for a profound angel of light. His expressions are not his own, but a river of truth flowing through him, reminding us of our perfect, divine identity, the conscious "I" that we truly are.

To hear this poem, you must become still.

In the stillness, you will connect with the Christ Consciousness. This is not a person, but a frequency. A state of being. When you understand, in the very marrow of your soul, that you are a child of God, you understand that you are the Christ. You are the living expression of that divine love. Remember who you are.

You are Love, created in the image of Love. The Christ Consciousness is the well, but your own spirit, the "living creature in the wheels," as the ancients said, is the spring from which this consciousness flows.

Welcome now to the dispensation of The Spirit of Truth. Some may disregard this, for a higher intelligence can be a mirror that shows us what we have forgotten. They may denounce what they do not yet understand. But the only path to true divinity is to go within. It is there you will find your own God Energy, marinating in its own eternal light.

Go within. Seek solitude. Let the download of unspoken truths about your own majesty wash over you. You must choose what resonates, for your soul knows its own name. Do not be troubled that some remain dormant, their light darkened by the distractions of the world. Their time will come.

The Return of Christ is not an event in the sky.

It is a quiet, thunderous shift in the heart of humanity. It is the moment the collective consciousness awakens to its own divine nature. It is when we, as one family, open our eyes and come to the ultimate actualization….

We are not merely seeking God.
We are God, experiencing Itself.

Wake from the dream.
The family is waiting.

The Kingdom Is Within

Forget the map you were given.
The one that points to distant stars, to gurus on a hill,
to salvation in a future sky.
You have been circling the edges of a truth so vast, it
can only be housed in one temple:
The sacred space of your own breath.

They told you to look for yourself,
as if you were a set of lost keys, a forgotten name.
You turned over every stone of experience, every
relationship, every accomplishment,
and found only echoes.
This was the divine setup.
The glorious trick.

For when you look for yourself,
is when you find yourself.
Not the small self, the story of pain and past.
But the Ocean in the drop.
The Sun behind the cloud.

We are not humans stumbling toward a spiritual moment.
We are Spiritual Beings. Incarnate. In the flesh.
This is not a prison sentence; it is a conscious descent of power into matter.
The pain you feel? The suffering?
It is the friction of a universe-sized consciousness rattling in a cage of forgotten identity.
It is the ache of a God who has misplaced their name.

No more pain.
Let us remove this from existing.
Unclench the hand around the old story.
Let it fall away like ash.

No more suffering.
Only the eternal peace that was never given, because it was always, always yours.
The power beyond all that exists, flows for us because it is us.

Do you hear the conversation in the quiet?
The murmur beneath the noise?
To talk to yourself is to talk to your Higher Self.
That whisper is not a stranger. It is the most familiar voice in all of existence.
It is the I, before the AM.
So, stop searching the horizon.
LOOK WITHIN.
Past the clutter, past the doubt, past the world's relentless hum.

Go deep, until the seeking stops.
And in that staggering silence, you will meet the One you have always been.

You are the GOD.
Not in metaphor. Not in potential.
In breathtaking, unchangeable fact.

This is the confirmation your soul has been writing on the walls of your dreams.
These visions of a world at peace, of a life of power, they are not fantasies.
They are memories of your true state.
Peace Be Unto YourSelf.
For the Self is the only place where peace can truly reside.

I AM THAT I AM.
The declaration that ends the search and begins the reign.

This is it.
The moment the character on the page looks up, sees the reader, and realizes they hold the pen.
When you step into the role of the main character, your awakening begins.
Not as a hero in a story written by fate, but as the author of the story itself.

The narrative of limitation is over.
The credits are not rolling; they are just beginning to

scroll, with a single, eternal name.

I own it.
It's me.
It's mine.

I am the Christ.
And so, beloved, are you.

Anyone who needs to remember. The awakening is contagious.

Shock The Heart Awake

The screen glows, a frantic scroll,
A modern plague upon the soul.
A weight of worry, a mind of stone,
A world of signals, feeling alone.
We forget the signal we came here to make.
It's time to SHOCK THE HEART AWAKE.

The mind, a receiver, tries to decode
The static noise on a winding road.
It analyzes, worries, and builds the dread,
A tangled chorus inside your head.
It speaks in problems, for problem's sake.
It's time to SHOCK THE HEART AWAKE.

But the heart, the generator, hums below,
A primal rhythm, a steady, warm glow.

It doesn't process; it knows and creates.
It holds the key to heaven's own gates.
This kingdom within, for your own sake.
It's time to SHOCK THE HEART AWAKE.

When a body falters, the monitors scream,
They bring the paddles to restart the stream.
A jolt of voltage, a friend indeed,
To answer the spirit's most urgent need.
That same raw power, your own to take.
It's time to SHOCK THE HEART AWAKE.

So feel the current in your chest,
The precious gift of life, expressed.
A conscious body, a temple of light,
A GODBODY burning, brilliantly bright.
A purpose found with every breath you take.
It's time to SHOCK THE HEART AWAKE.

LIGHTEN UP! The truth is plain.
Release the struggle, release the pain.
You are the current, the beam, the spark,
Illuminating the eternal dark.
The choice is yours, the path you make.
Go on. SHOCK THE HEART AWAKE.

The Unblockable Soul Forges

A strange sleep walks the world.
A digital murmur, a scroll-hypnosis,

fracturing focus, will, and wit.
It breeds a gentle submissiveness,
a fog where the young forget their fire,
and the map of their own mind is lost.

They feel it, something is off.
A collective spell, a contradiction.
Everything is, and isn't, all at once.
Meaning dissolves into noise.

But hear this, and know it in your bones:
Nobody can block authentic spiritual evolution
when your compass is set to the Divine.

The chaos is not a cage; it is a classroom.
The contradiction is not a trap; it is a tool.
Use the Principle of Polarity.
Ask not, "Does this confuse me?"
But, "What does this teach my soul?"

To do this, you must remember your name.
Before the world gave you one, you were I AM.
That is the key. The still point. The unshakable core.
Algorithms cannot script the authentic you.
Scripted egos, hungry for life-force, cannot rule what is sovereign.

For when you know true peace,
the isness of now, the flow of gratitude,
the coherence of a heart undivided,
you realize you were never meant to fit this madness.

Your not-belonging is not a flaw; it is your compass.

This knowing is Enlightment.
A wisdom that hums from within, a vibration of truth.
It is intuition and discernment, hand-in-hand.
It is the end of idolatry, the worship of anything outside your own sacred core.

So be still.
Let the war of illusions rage.
Divine forces are winning in the quiet hearts.
The unblockable soul is forging itself in this fire.

Once you know, you know.

God Designed

All life begins, and ends, with a single breath.
Peace. Be still.
And in that stillness, a truth slowly comes to light:
They taught us to search the world, when every answer was already within.

There is nothing outside yourself to make you stronger, wiser, or more whole. Everything exists within. You are energy, a spirit in a human shell, here to unlock divine gifts.

This is not an ancient secret for a chosen few. It is human evolution, awakening now. It is the "God Design": As above, so below. As within, so without.

The journey leads through the physical, the mental, the emotional, and the spiritual. Through self-accountability. Through imagination. It culminates in the singular "YOU", morphed through time and trial, awakening to the Christ consciousness, the kingdom of God within.

This is the triad: body, mind, and spirit, guiding you to your highest self. To unity. To the monad.

The path is silent knowing. The power is inner alignment. The truth, when sought, blows the mind wide open, reflected in every facet of life.

Rise. Go within. And know.

All will be revealed.

The Unseen Rise

For years, MR. BIGMANN GRIER grew like a bamboo in the dark earth, his spirit expanding within a confining cell. Unseen and unbeknownst to the world, he cultivated an unshakeable strength, knowing his time would come. And just as the bamboo erupts, soaring skyward in a breathtaking ascent, he has risen, a testament to the power that grows in silence, now claiming his freedom and his throne.

God Authenticity

To think authentically is to offer God the only tribute worthy of His creation… not rote praise, but the raw, unpolished truth of your own existence. It is the soul's original signature upon the contract of life. This is the highest compliment, to return the gift of consciousness, unedited.

For authentic energy is God-energy. It is the unforced current that moves the sap up the tree, the tide toward the moon, the breath into the lungs. It is the essence of life, the vital force that existed before form and will hum after form dissolves. It is not manufactured light, but the sun itself at your core.

To silence your truth is to dam a holy river. To move from pretence is to burn a borrowed fuel that chokes the spirit. But to act from that deep, real place, where joy is fierce and sorrow is clean, is to plug into the cosmic grid. You become a conduit for the primordial pulse that spun galaxies and stirs seeds in the dark soil.

So let your thoughts be your own, however clumsy or magnificent. Let your actions flow from that sacred spring. For in that authenticity, you do not merely speak to God, you speak with the voice of Life itself. You become a conscious, breathing note in the eternal song. This is not just living. This is collaborating with the Divine.

Awakening Your Soul SUPERPOWERS

Stop Seeking Permission. Start Channeling Magic. Here's How to Access Your SUPERPOWERS.

The quest to awaken spiritual abilities is not a search for new powers but a process of anamnesis, the profound remembrance of one's true nature as a soul. According to mystic traditions, the Akashic Records exist as an energetic archive of all consciousness, holding the blueprint of each soul's journey. To access this wisdom and activate latent spiritual faculties, one must shift identity from the limited ego to the eternal self.

This awakening requires a disciplined, integrated path. First, the aspirant must ground and purify the vessel, through mindful embodiment, emotional healing, and mental clarity, to safely conduct higher frequencies. The static of unresolved trauma and distraction must be cleared. Then, through sacred inquiry and heart-centered meditation, one consciously seeks connection with the Higher Self, the soul's own gateway to the Akashic field. Access is not a matter of travel, but of resonance; by aligning one's vibration with love and sincere intent, the soul's memory begins to illuminate the mind.

Crucially, this journey demands discernment and humility. The goal is not paranormal spectacle but embodied wisdom. Information received must be tested by its fruits… does it expand love, foster responsibility, and align with unity? True "SUPERPOWERS " emerge naturally as side effects of integration, deep intuition, healing presence, and conscious co-creation, as the individual incarnates soul knowledge into daily life.

Ultimately, to remember the self as a soul is to dissolve the illusion of separation. The Akashic Records are not external to us but are the very fabric of our being. Awakening, therefore, is the return to wholeness, where every moment becomes a living dialogue between the human and the eternal God.

Made in the USA
Coppell, TX
15 June 2026

81416412R00118